Birthday Bash

An Advanced Coloring Book

By

Sara Hickman

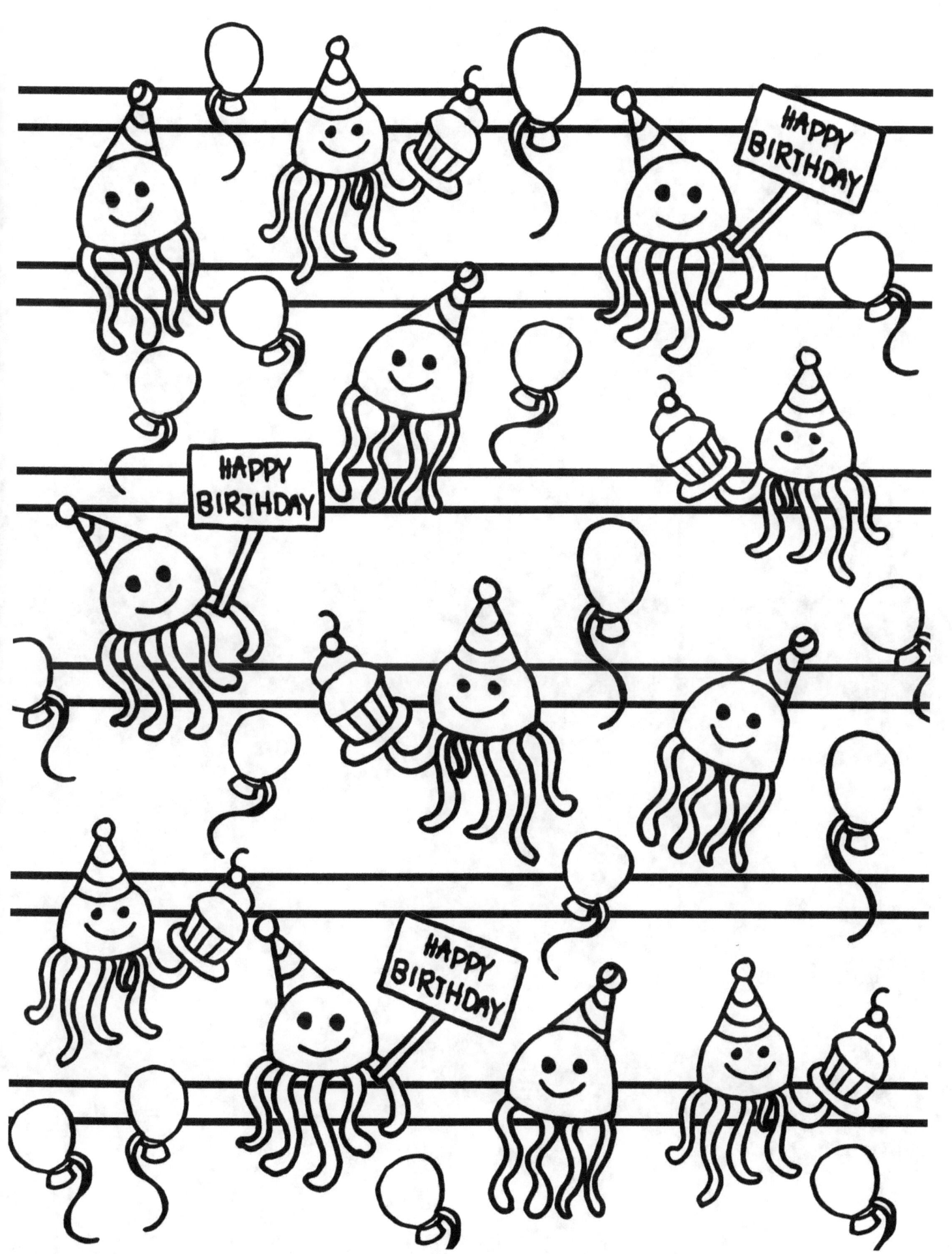

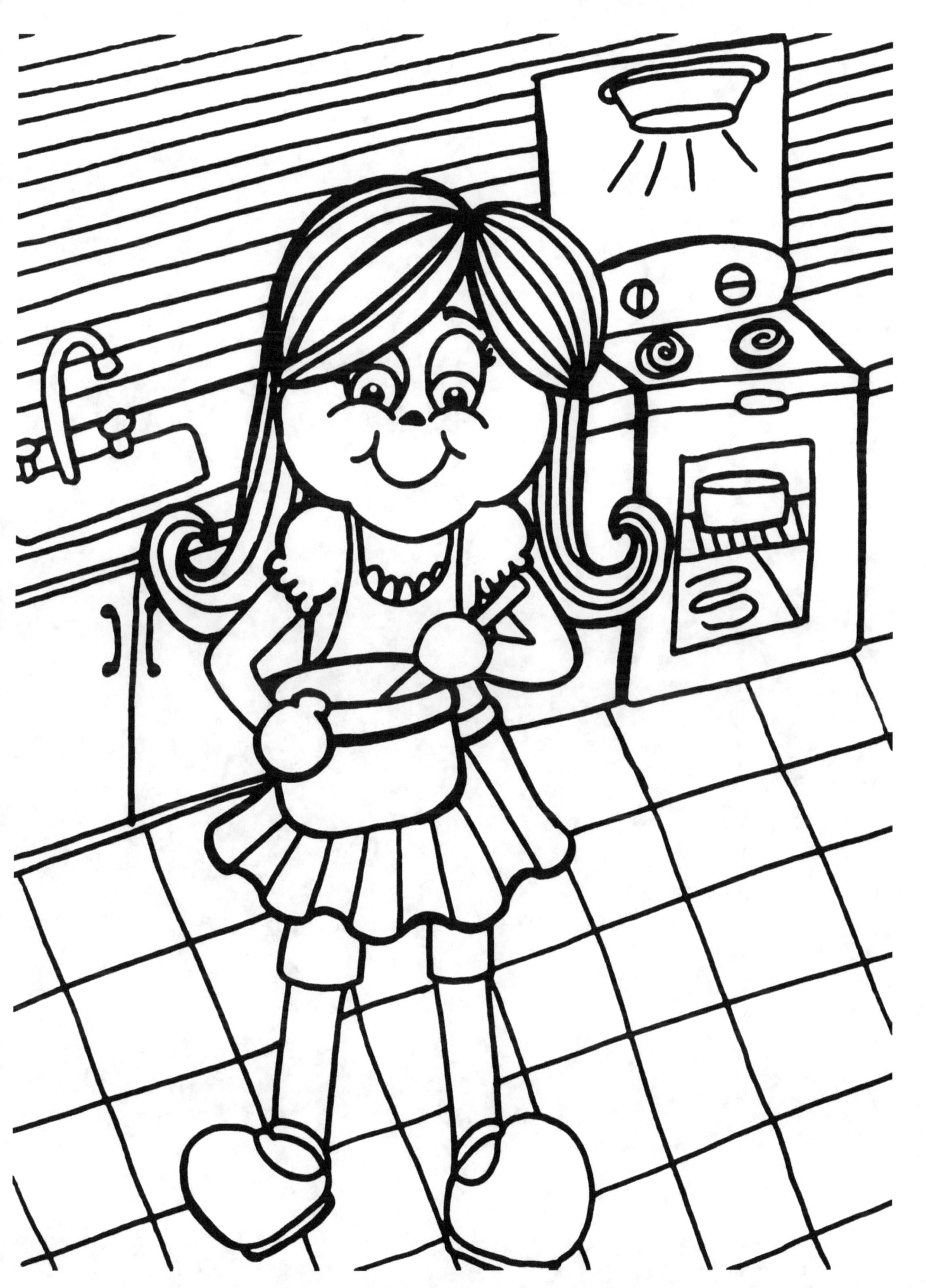

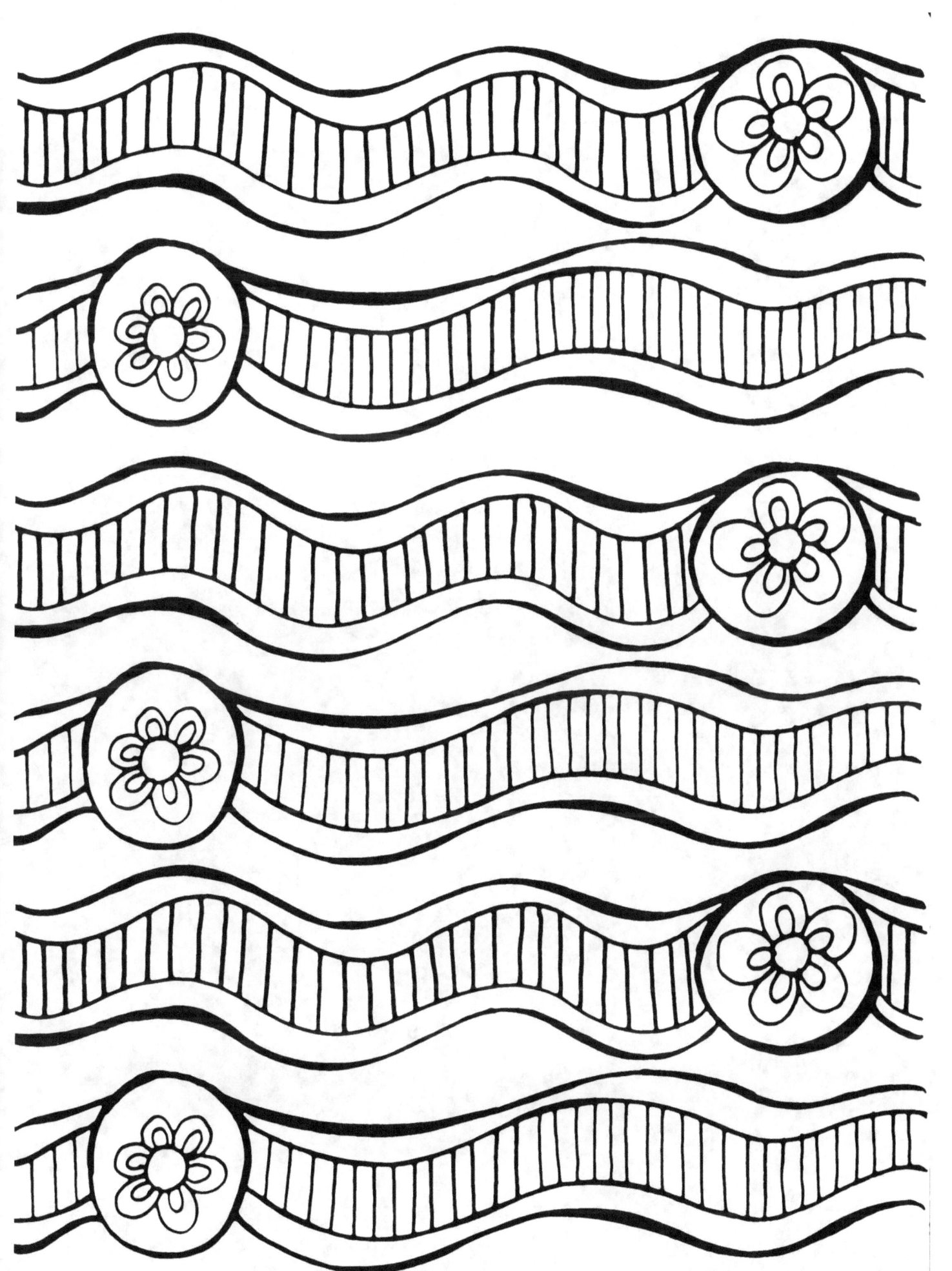

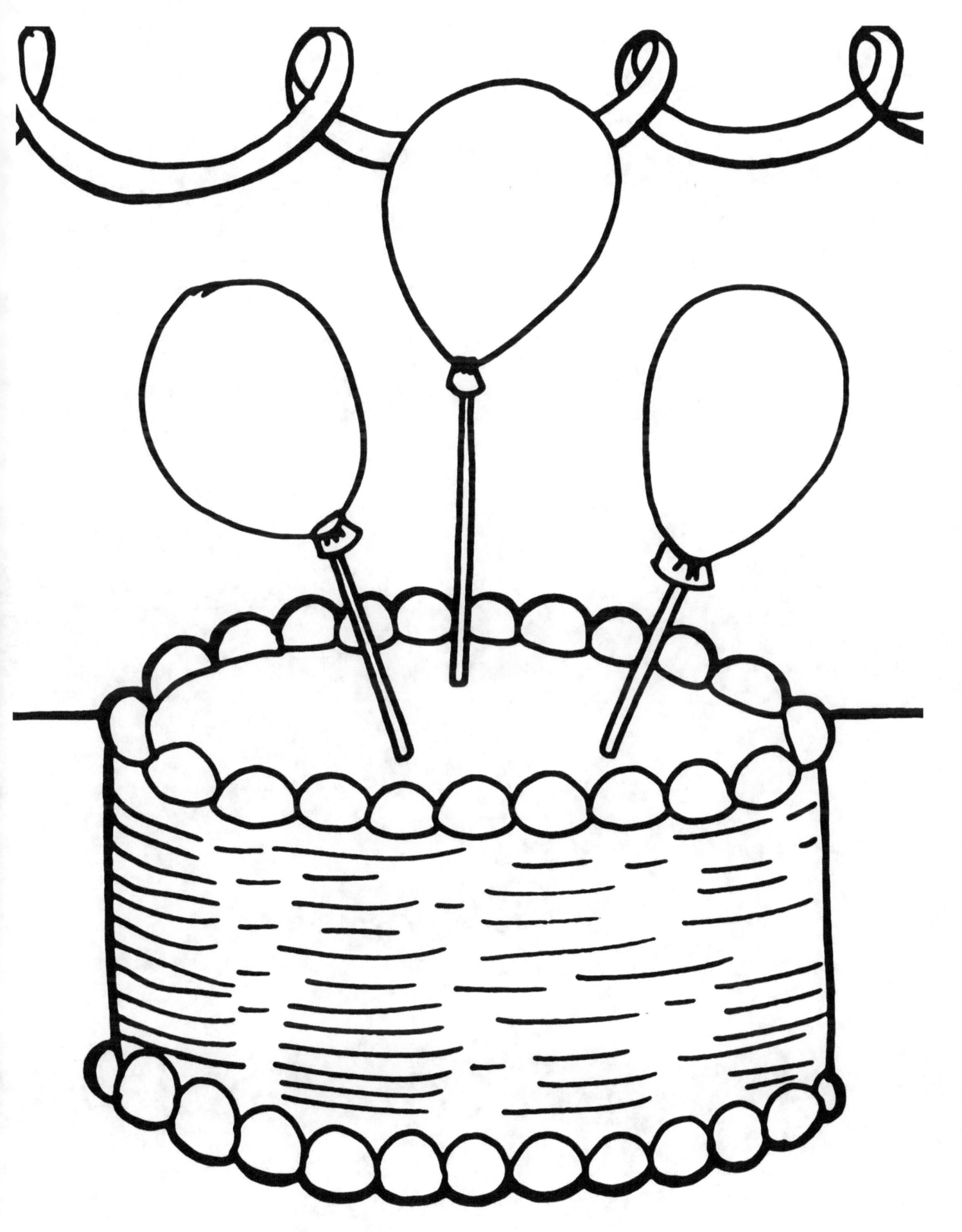

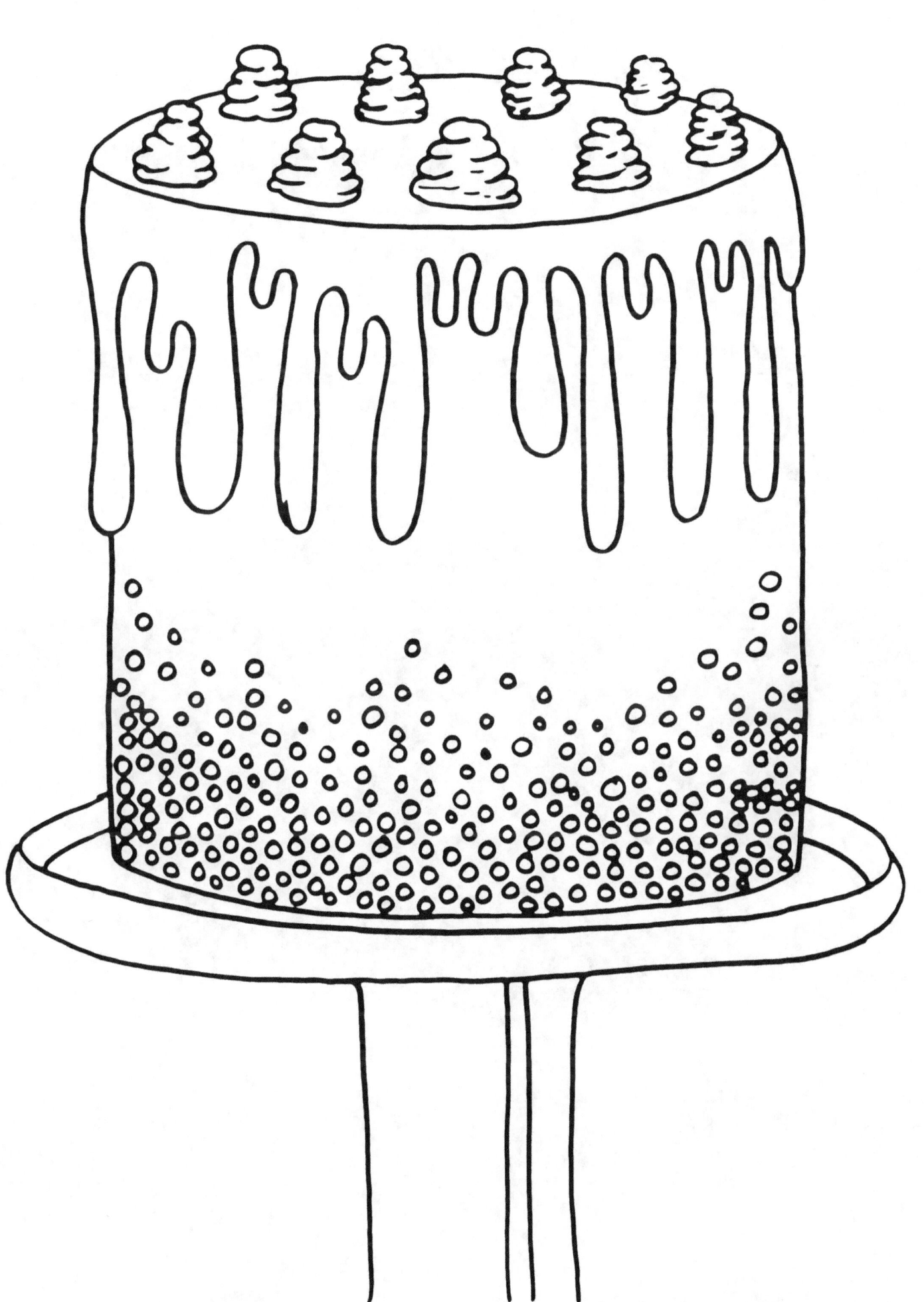

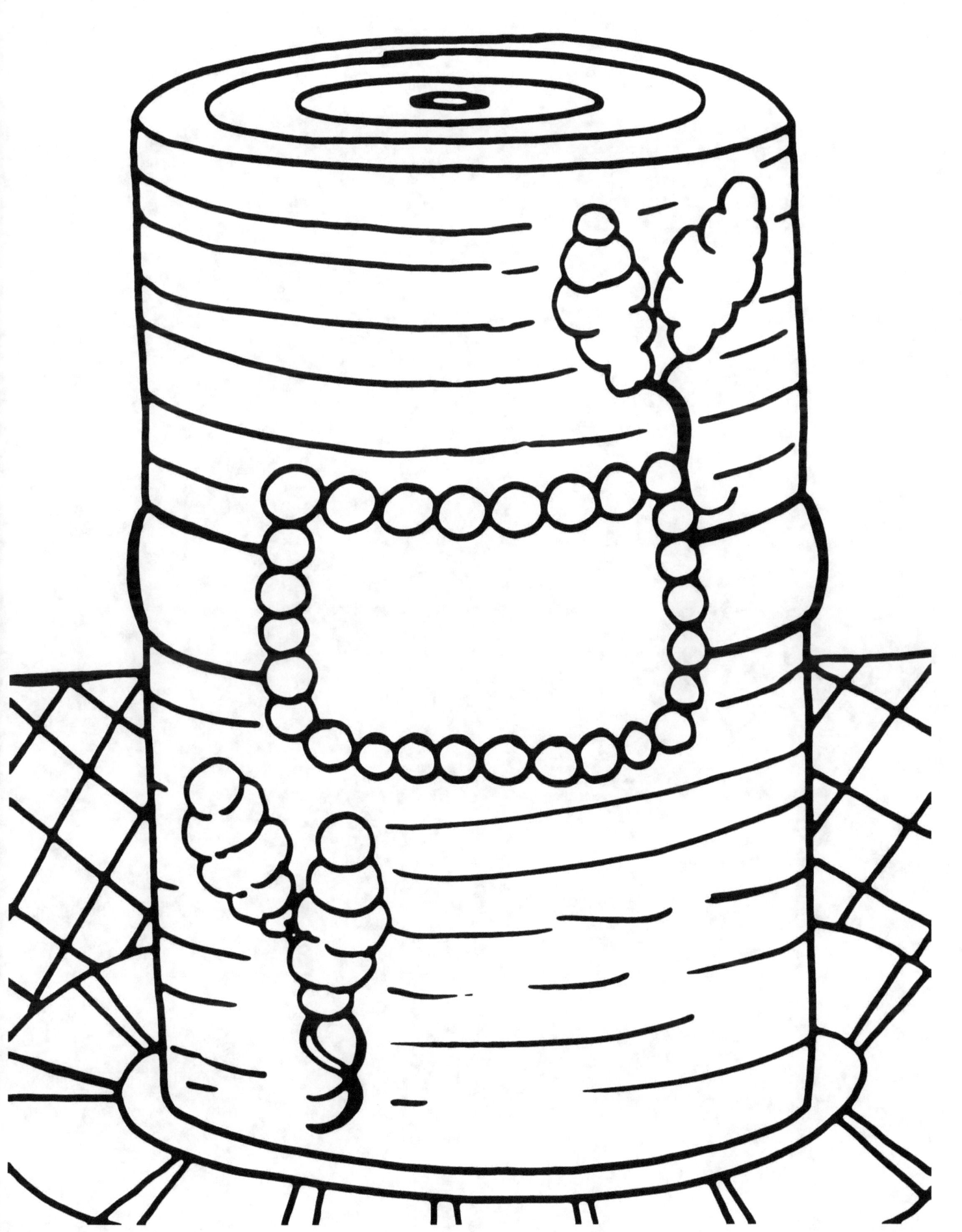

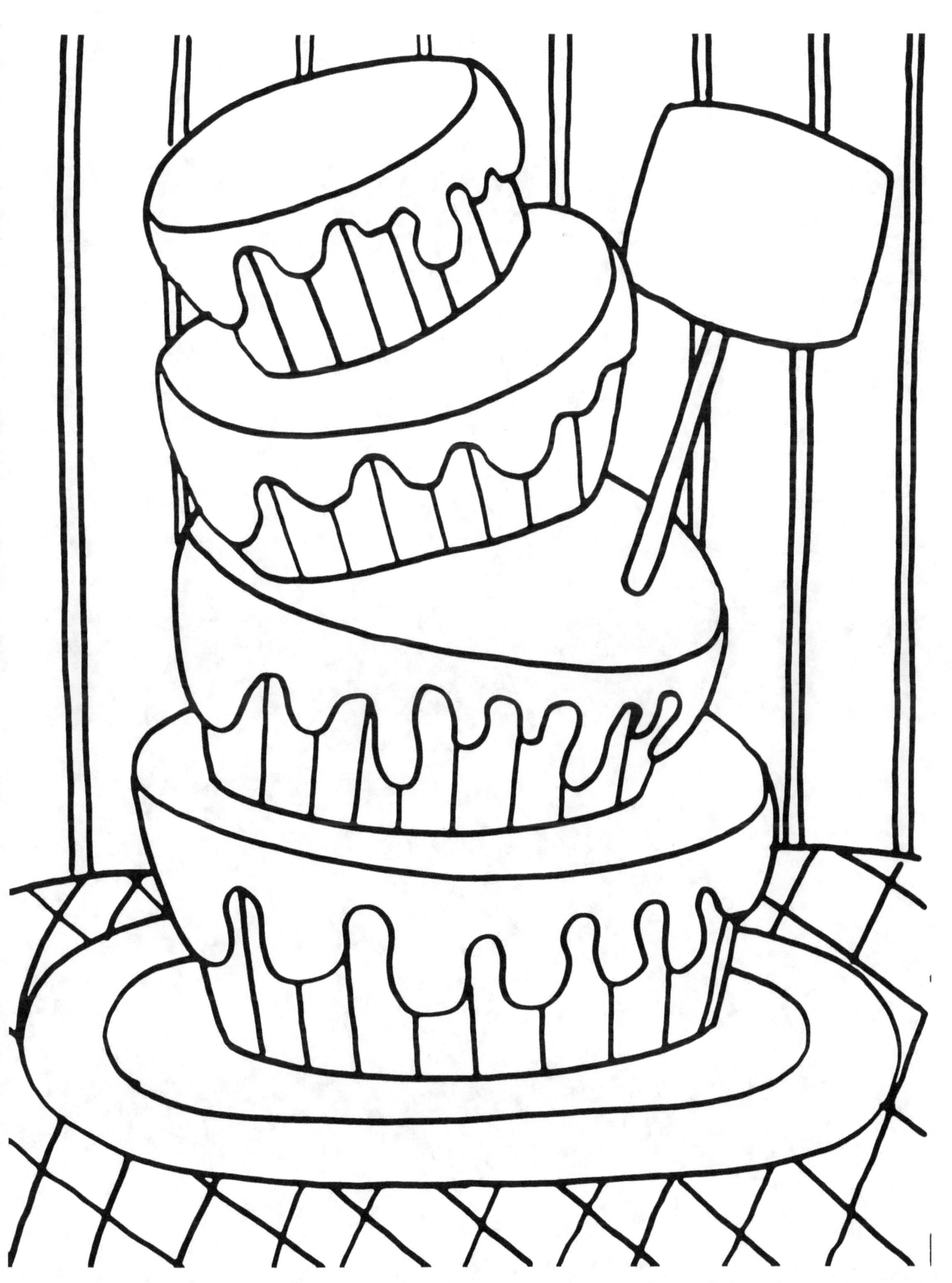

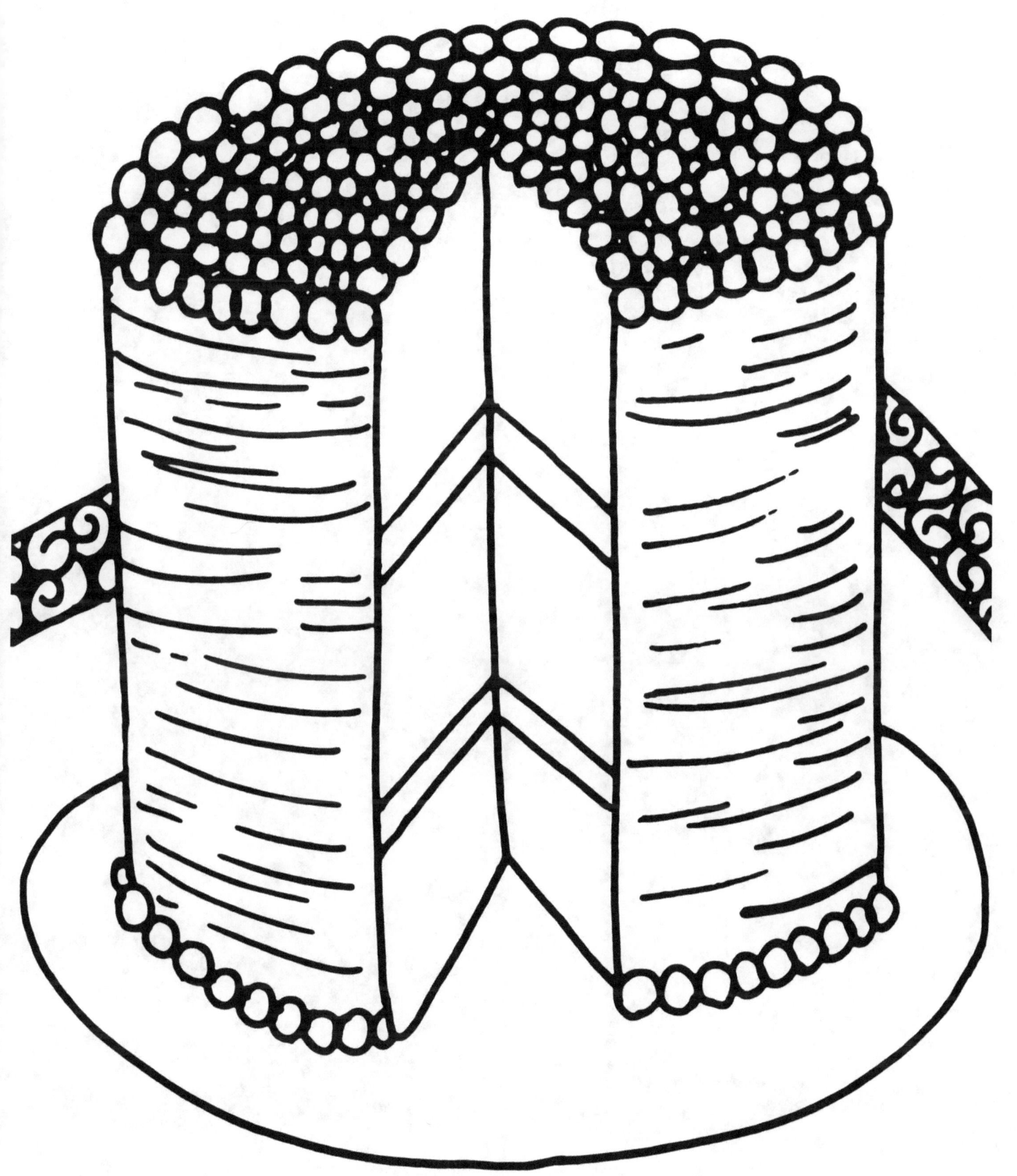

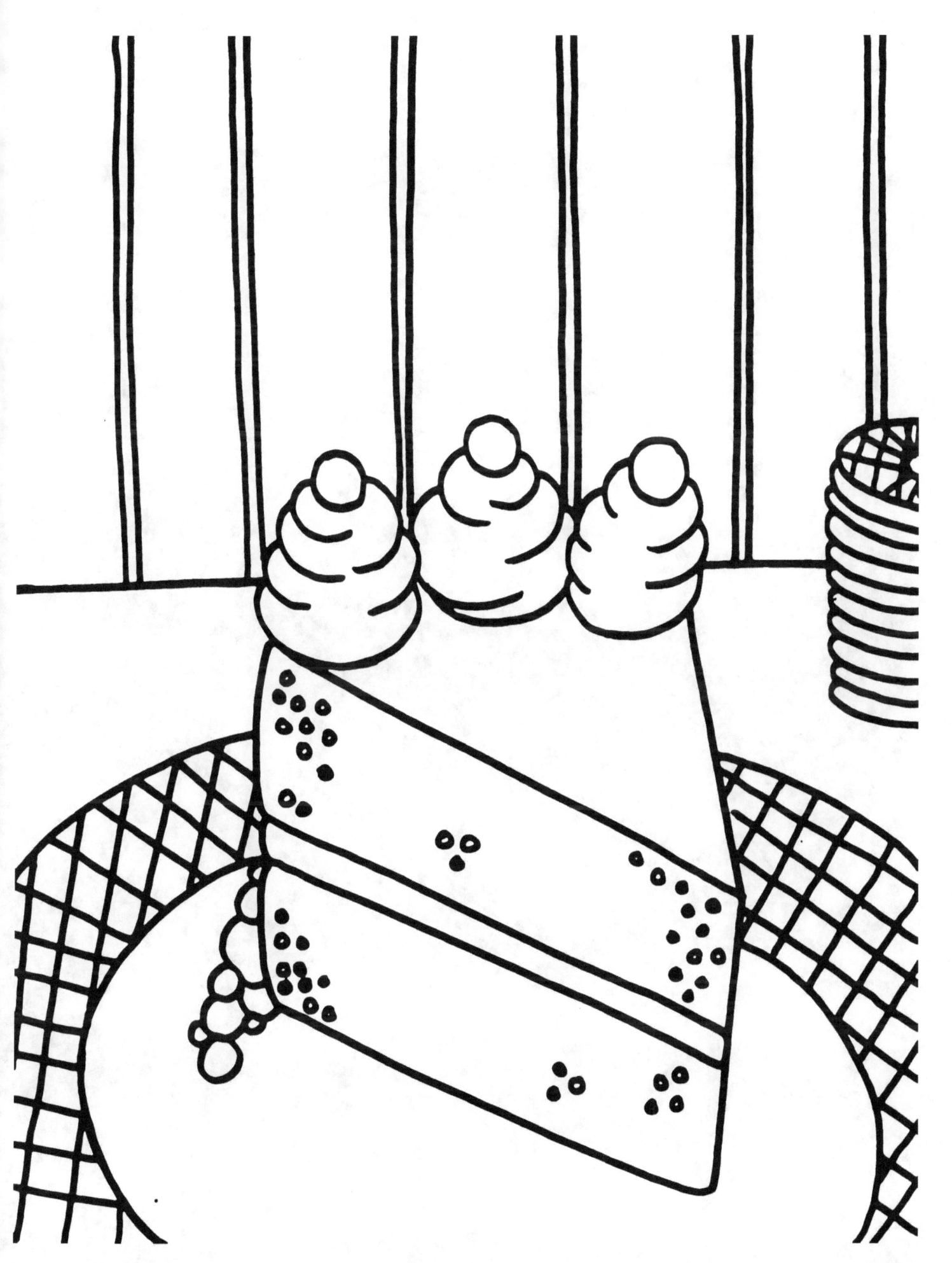

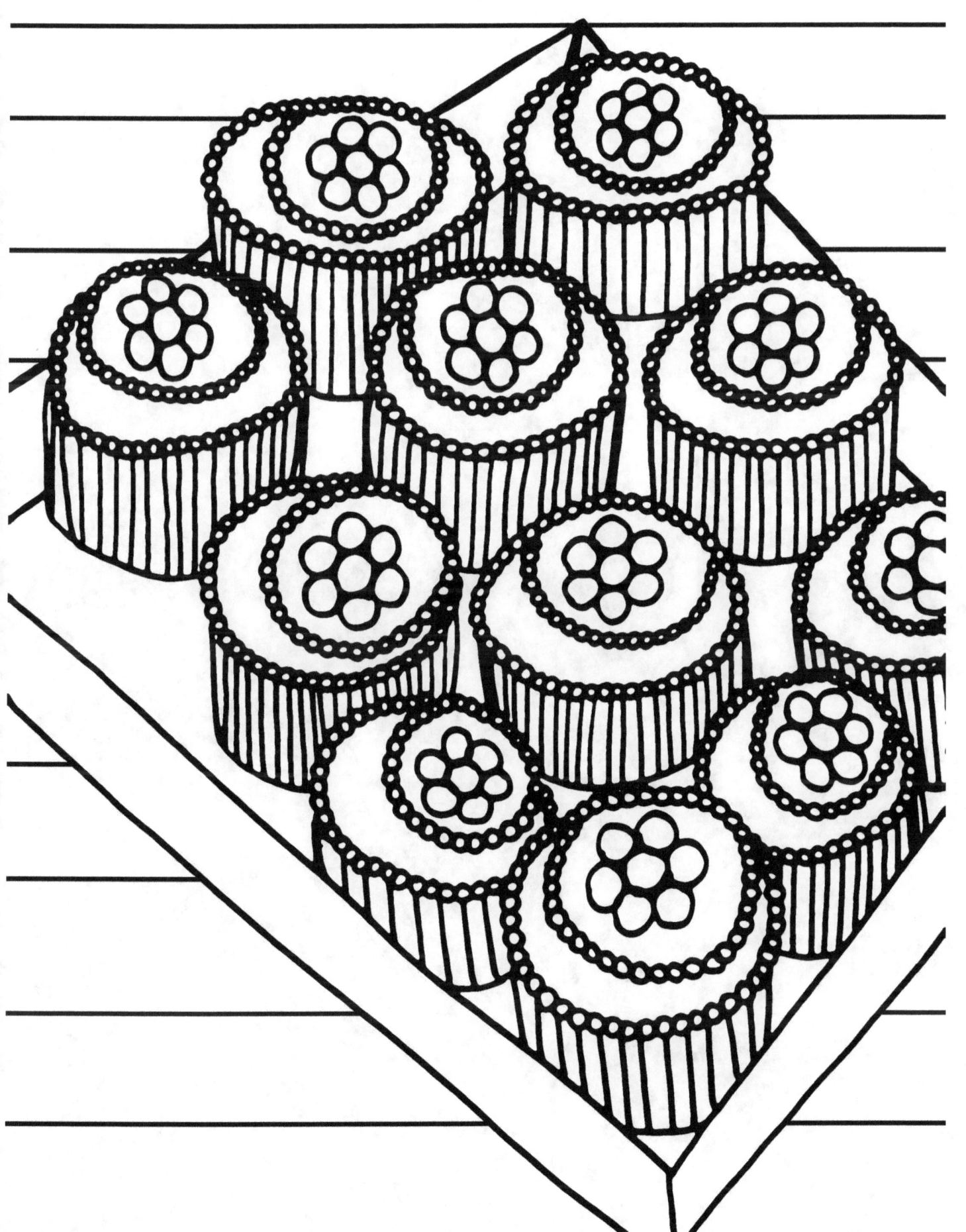

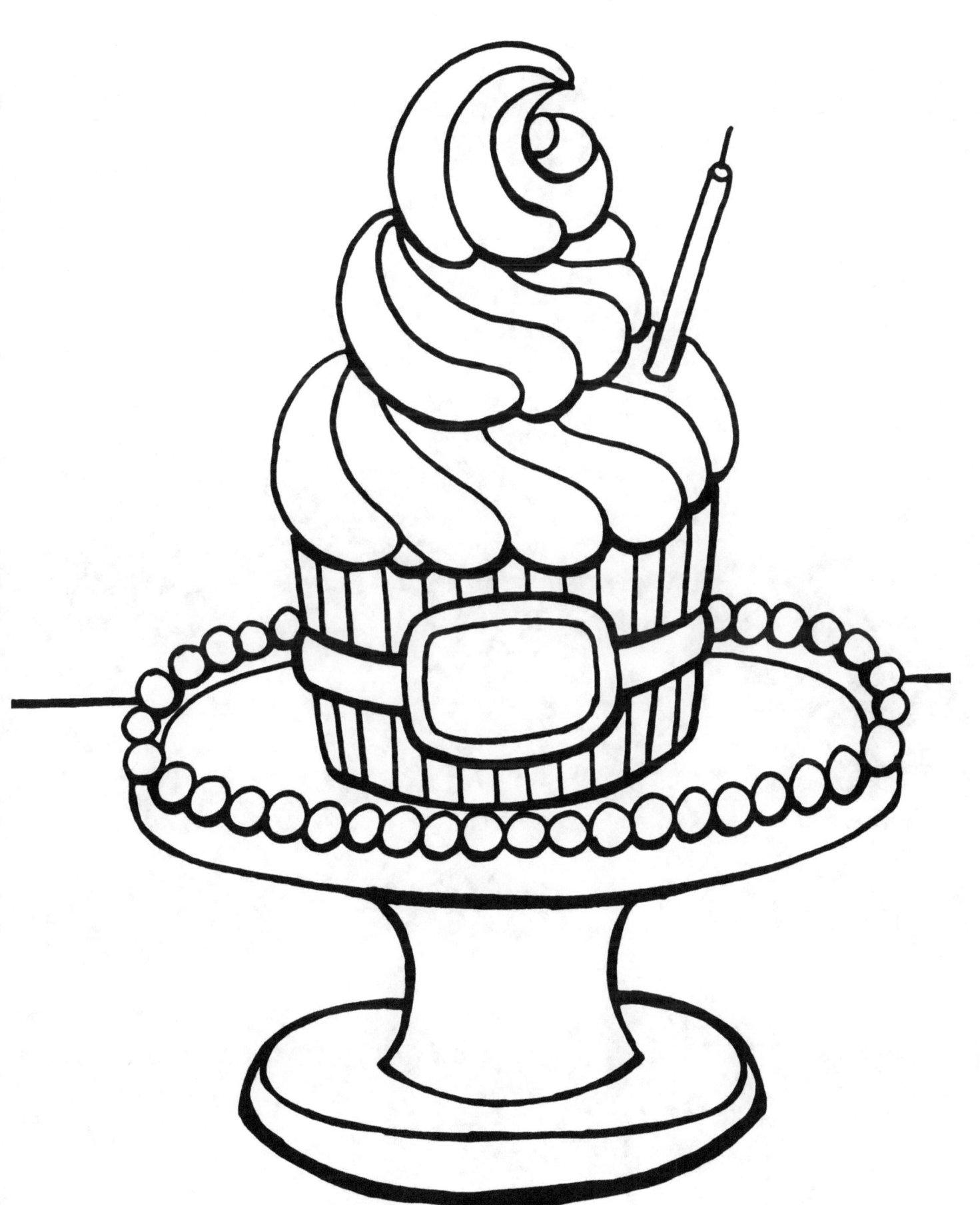

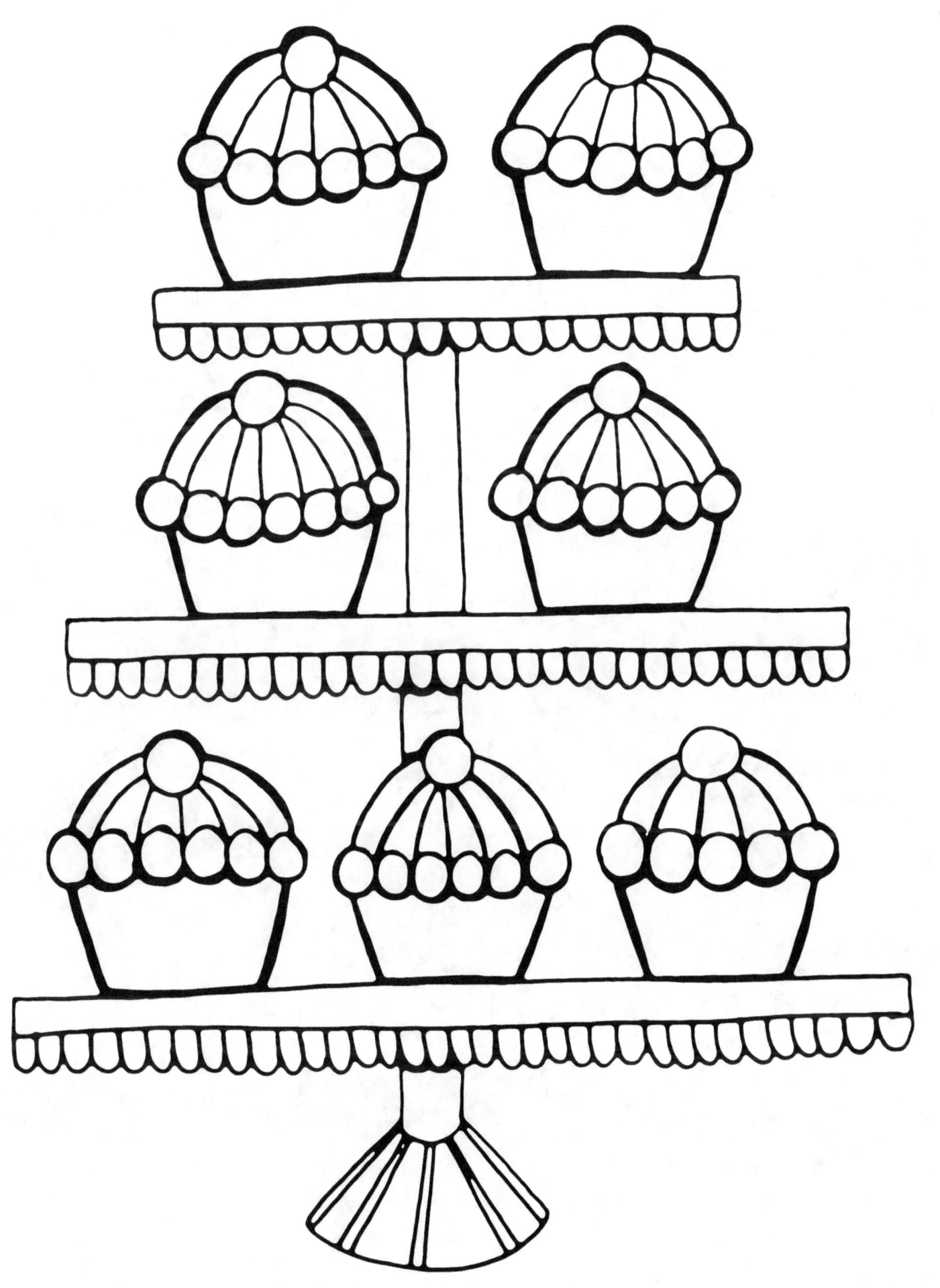

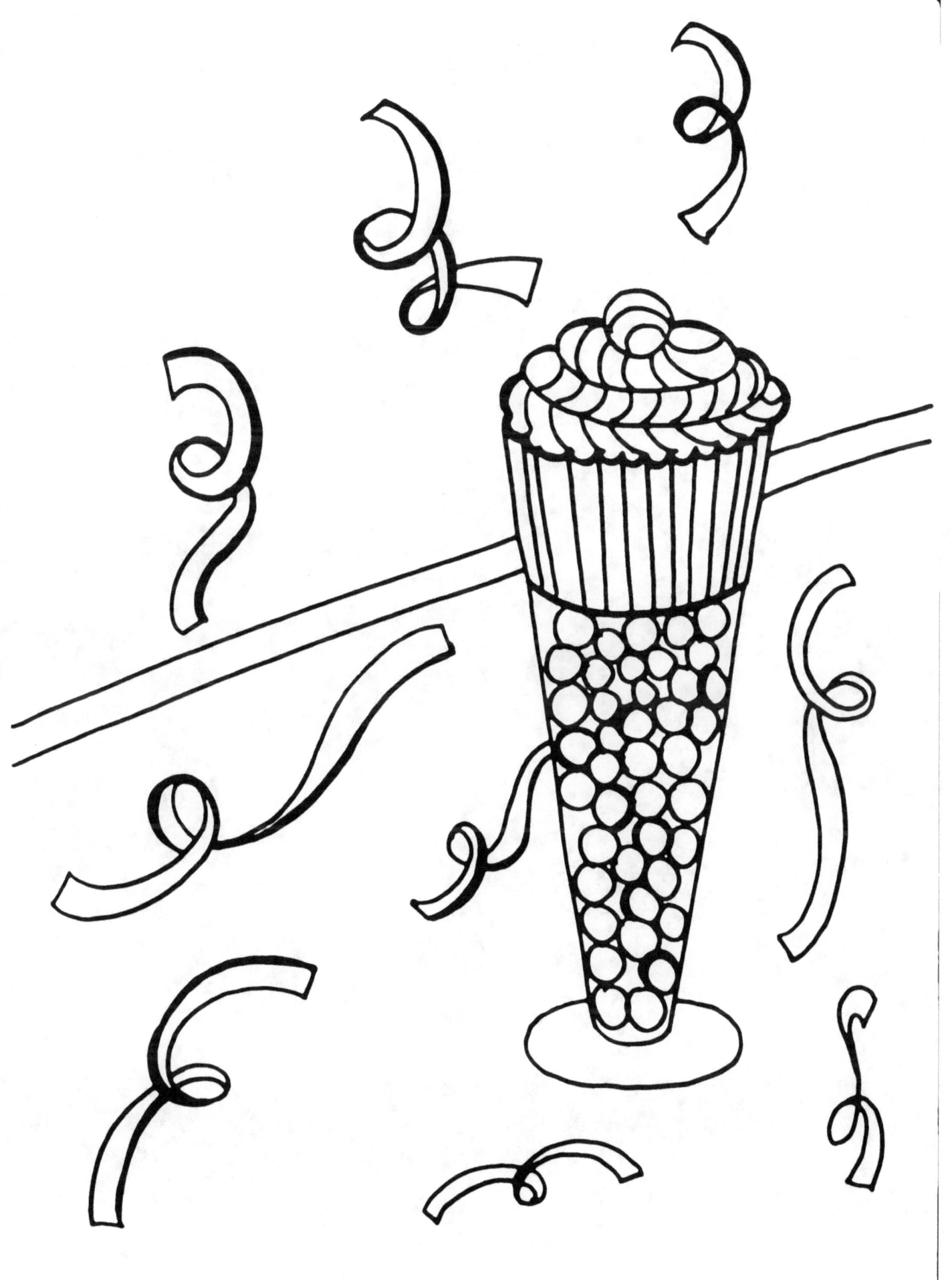

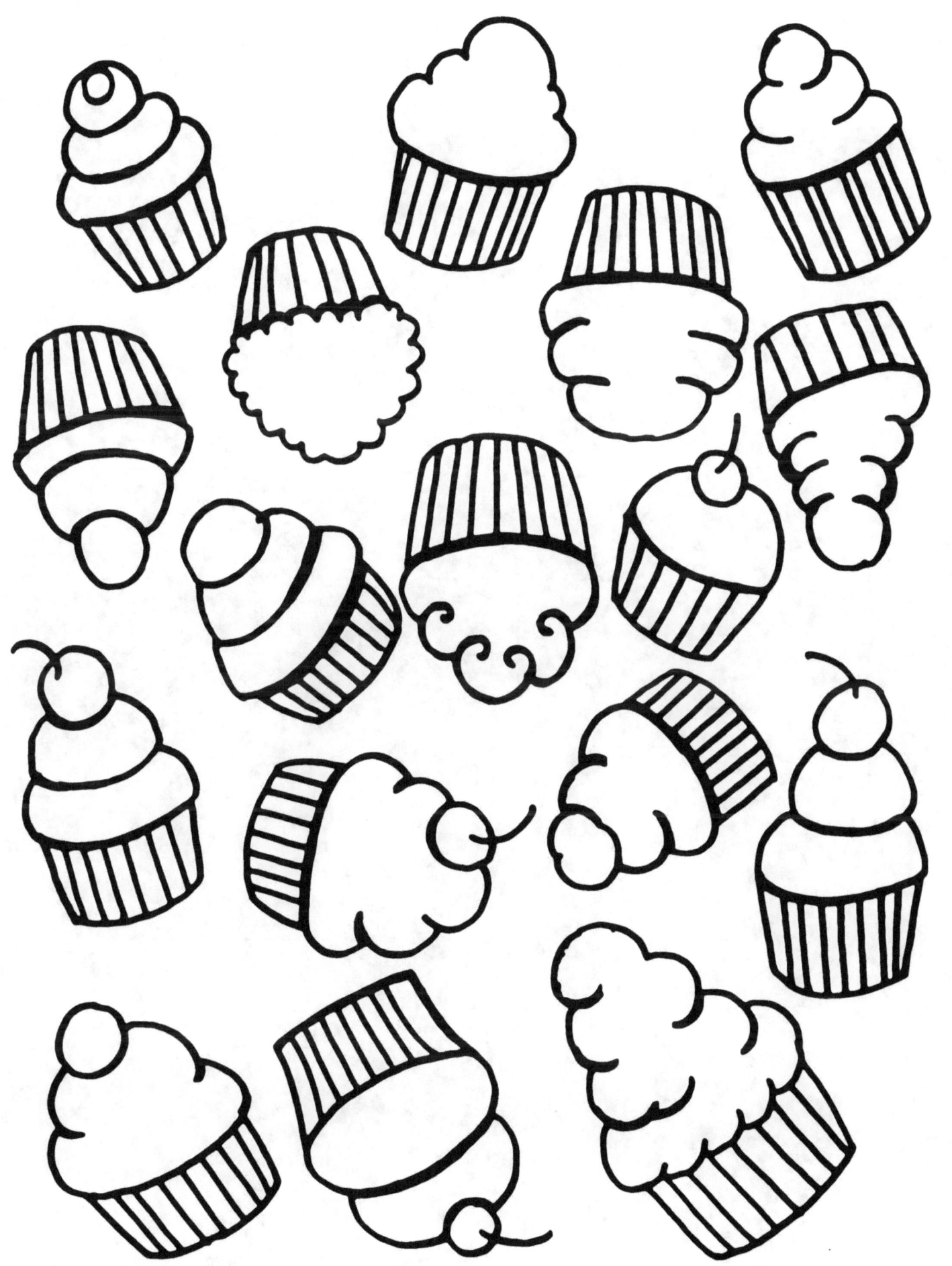

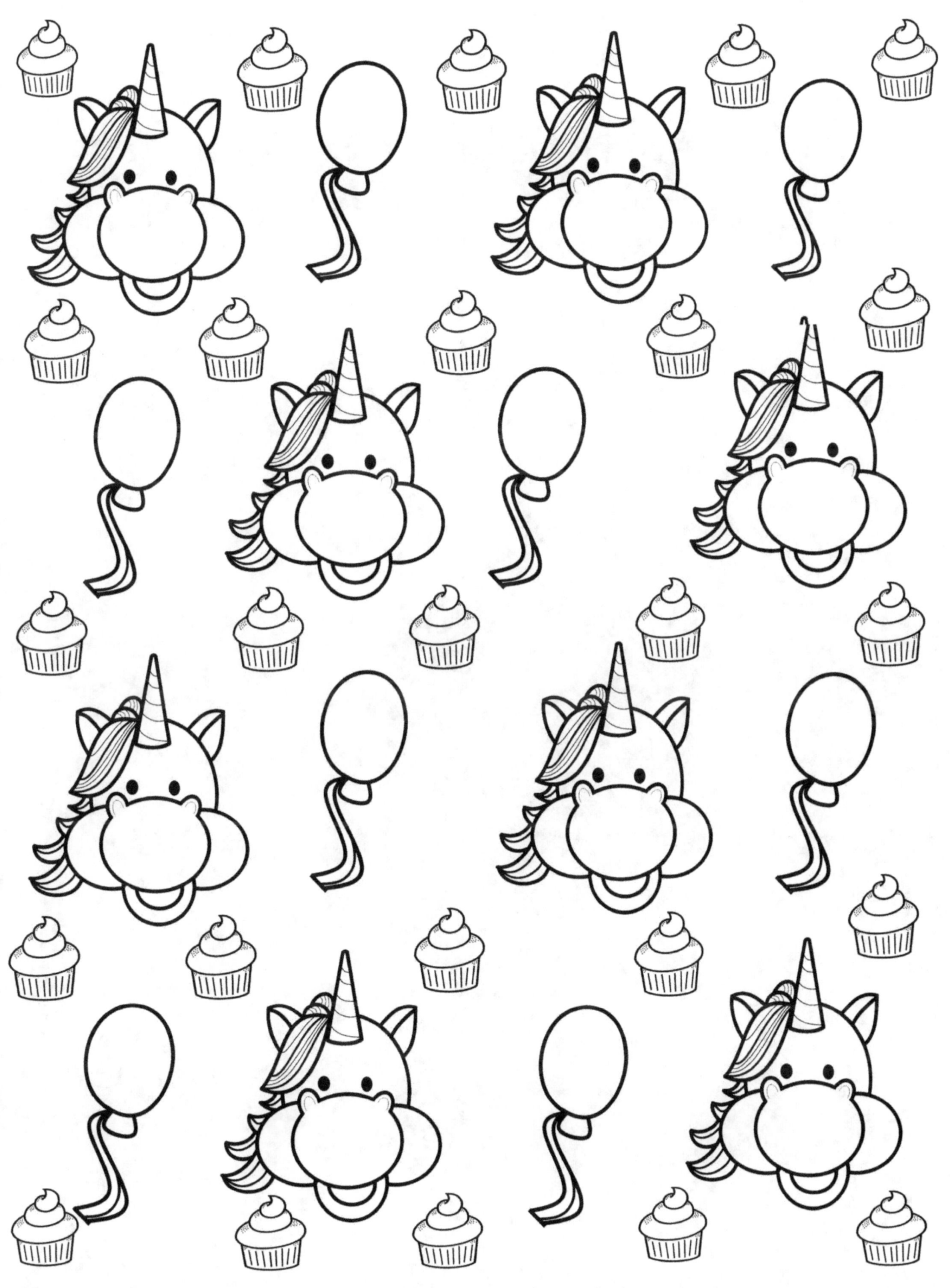

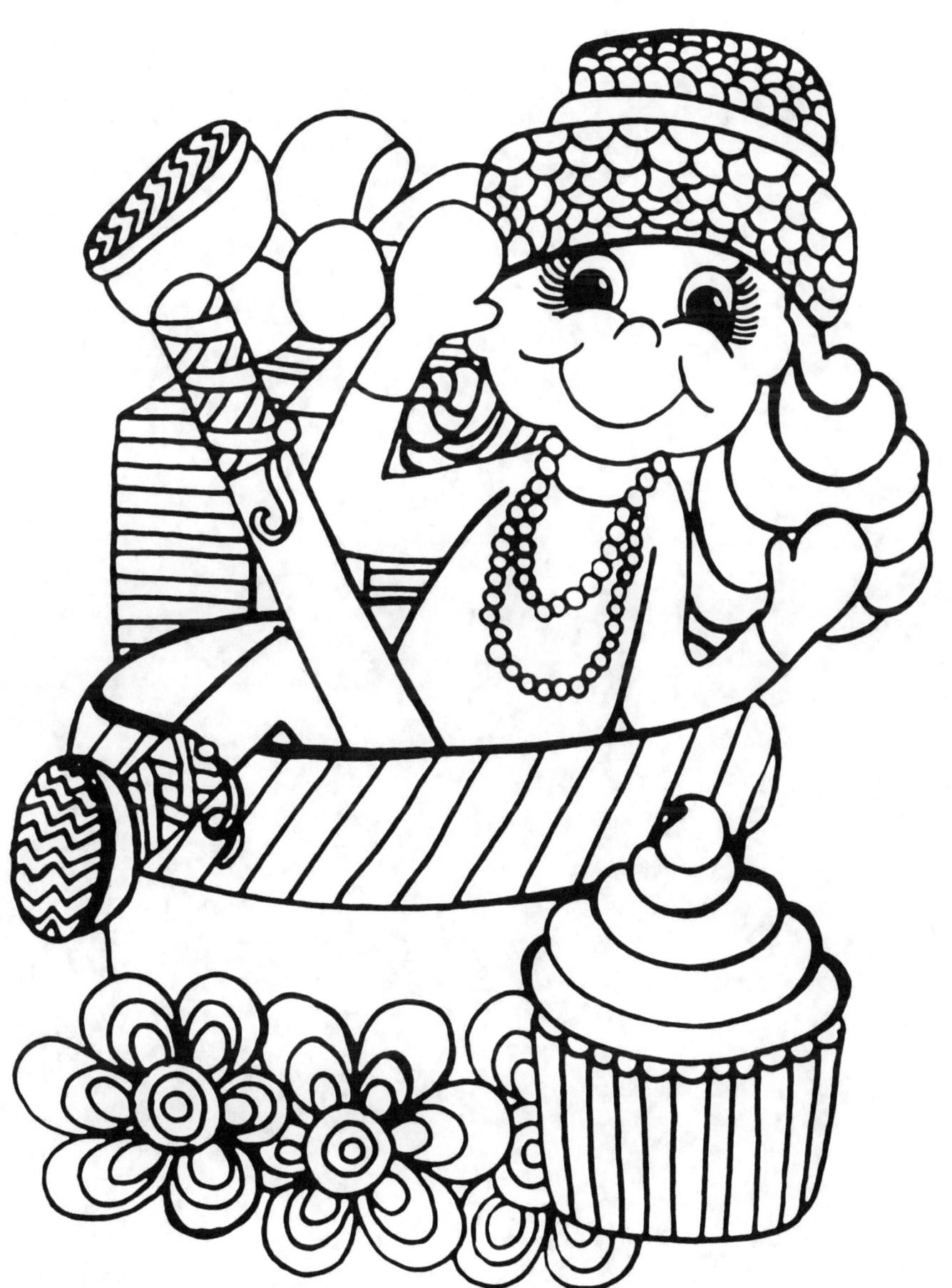

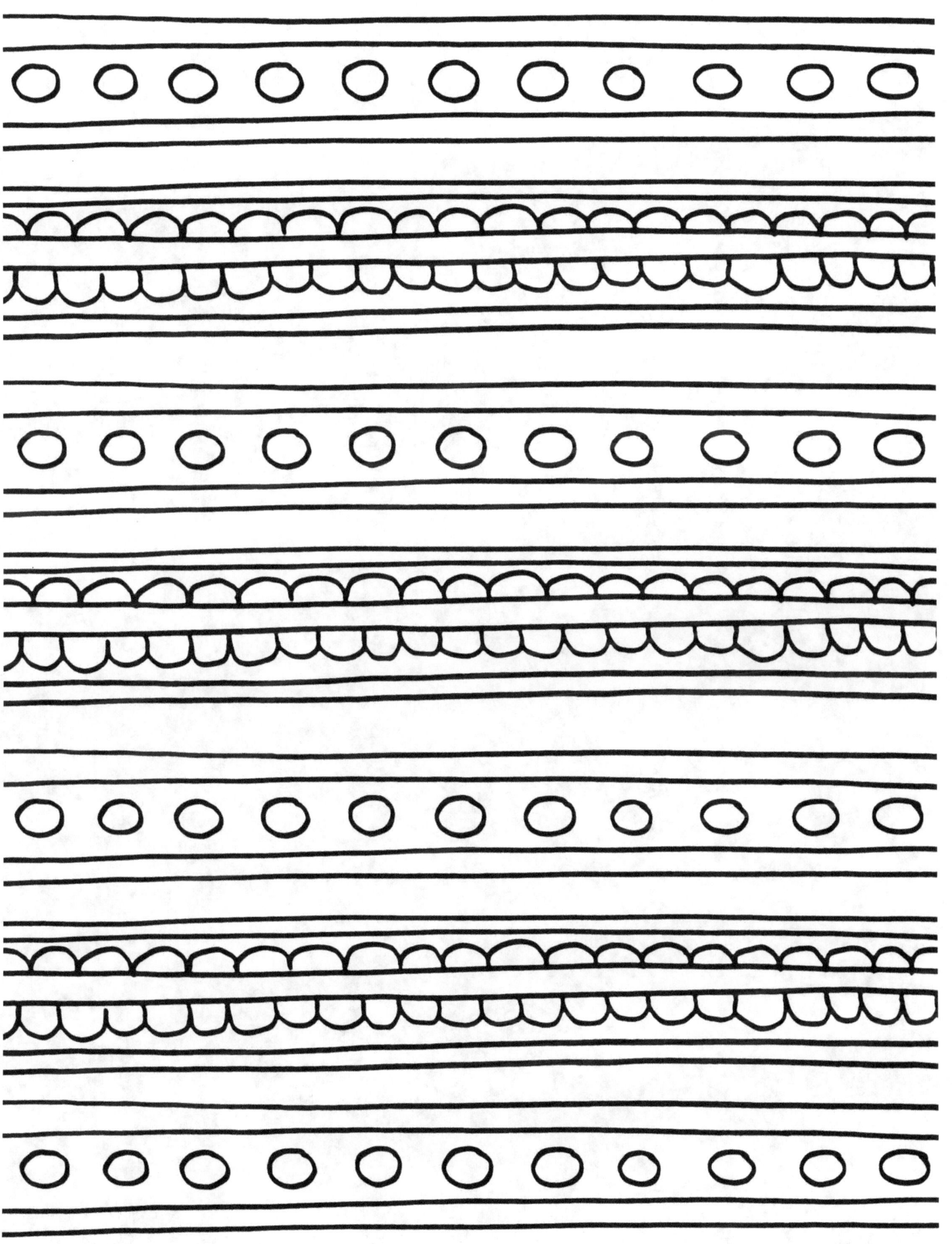

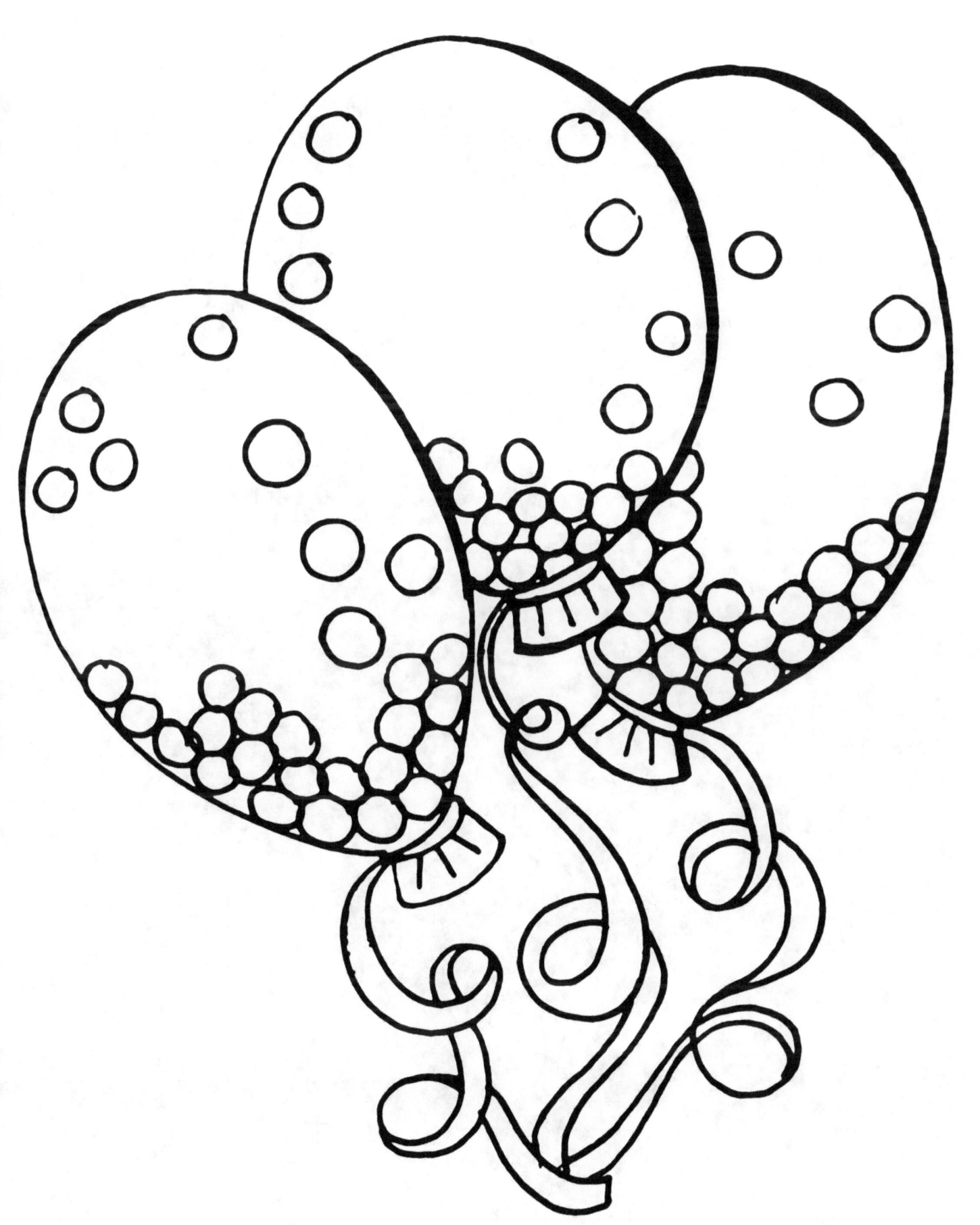

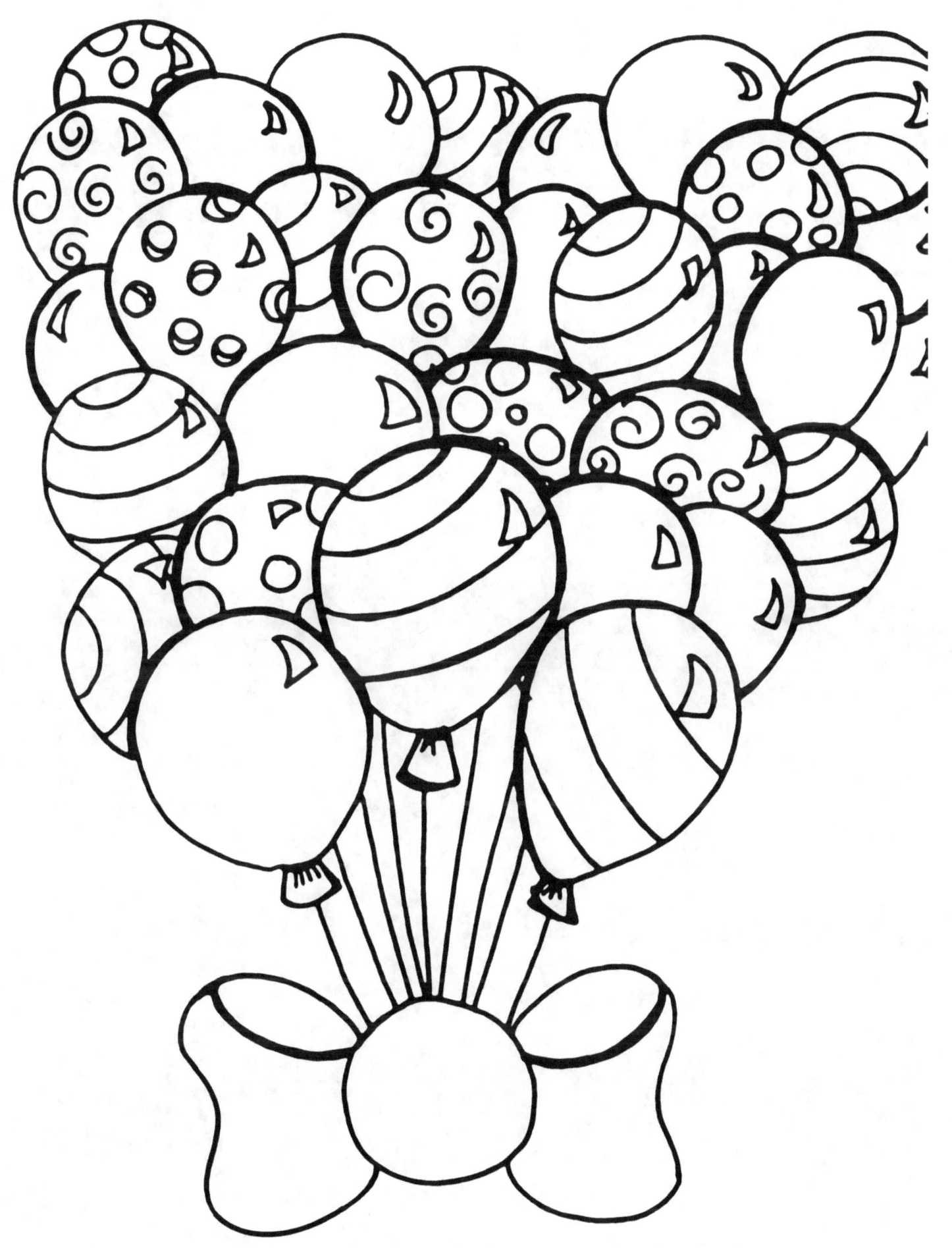

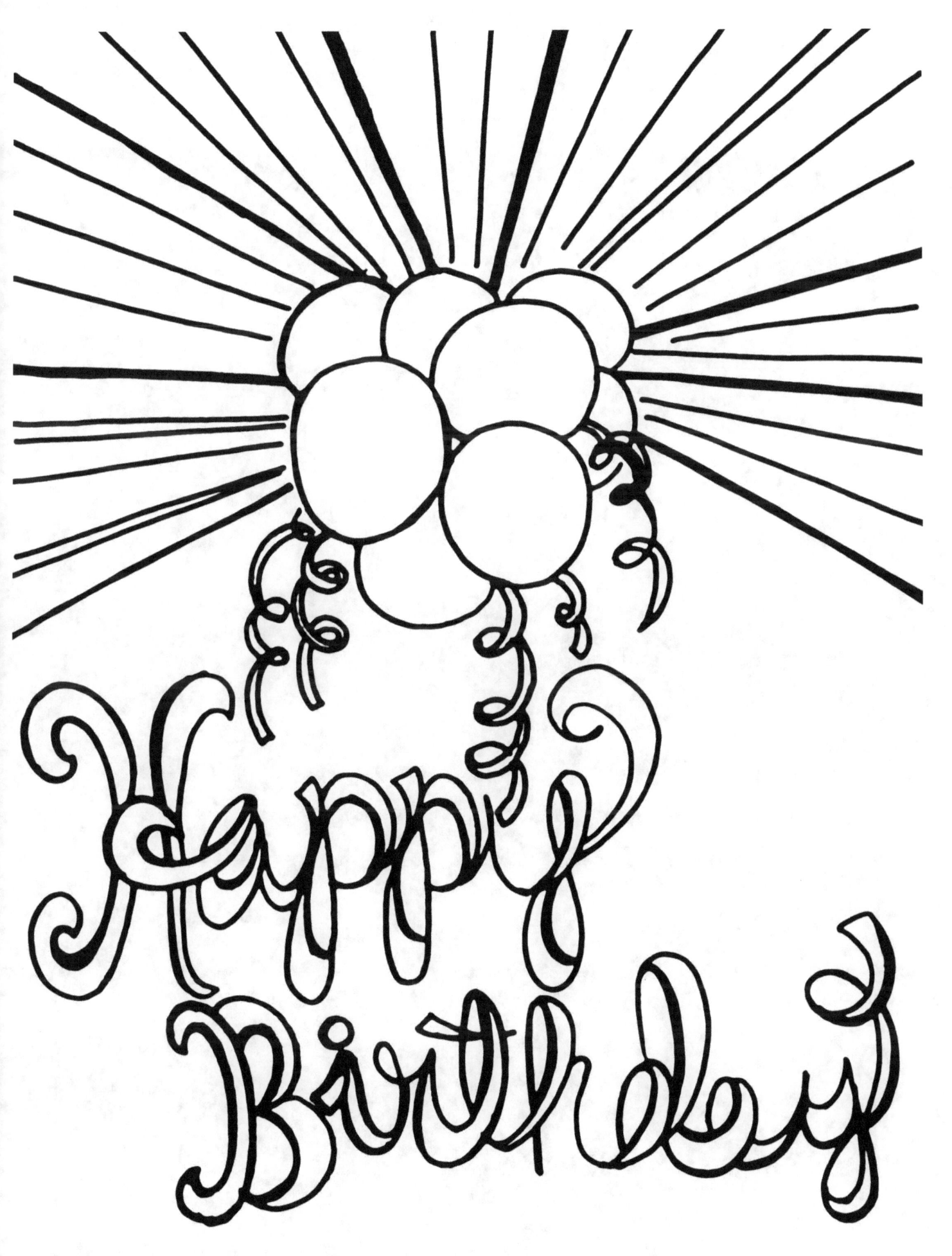

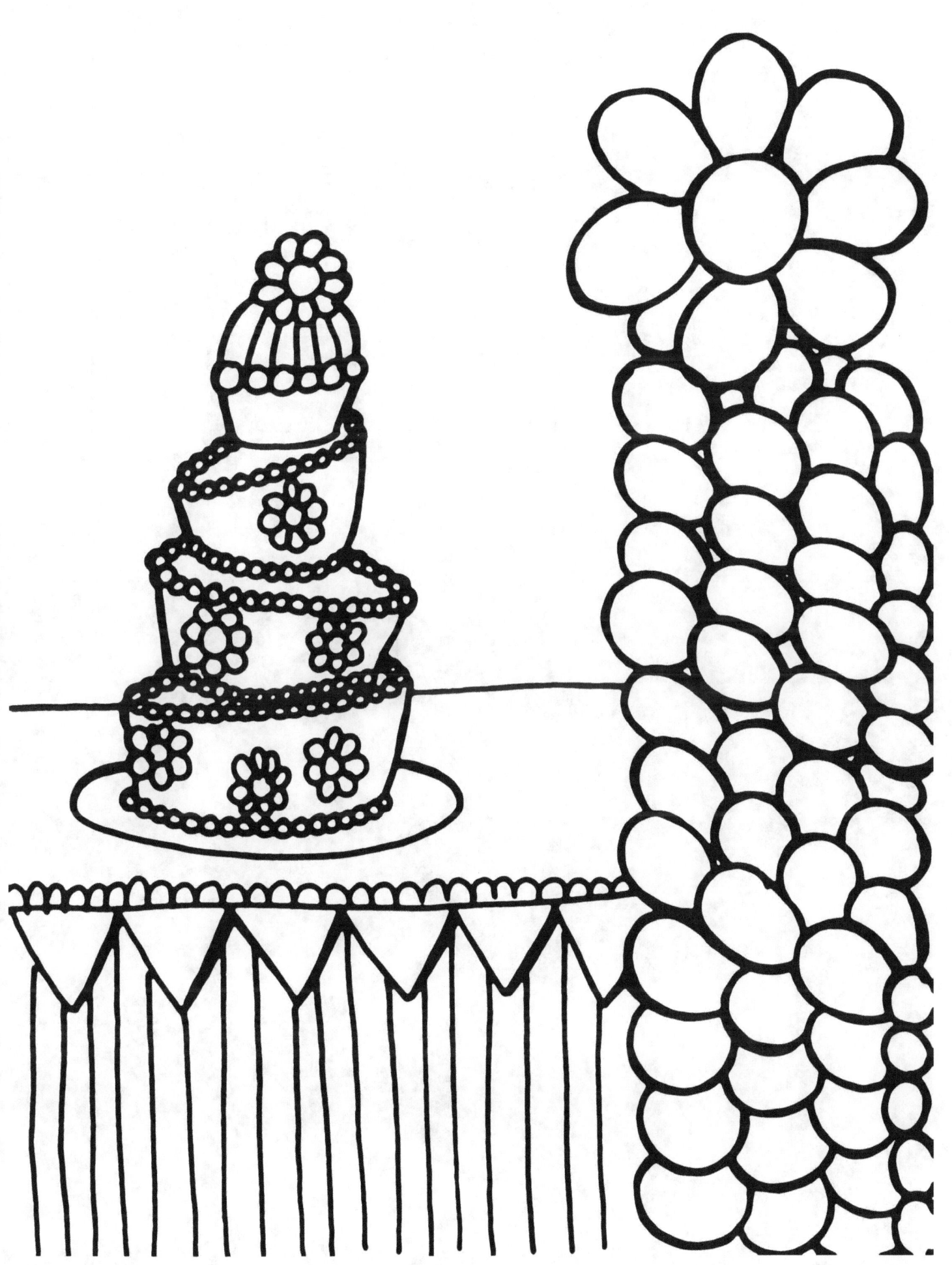

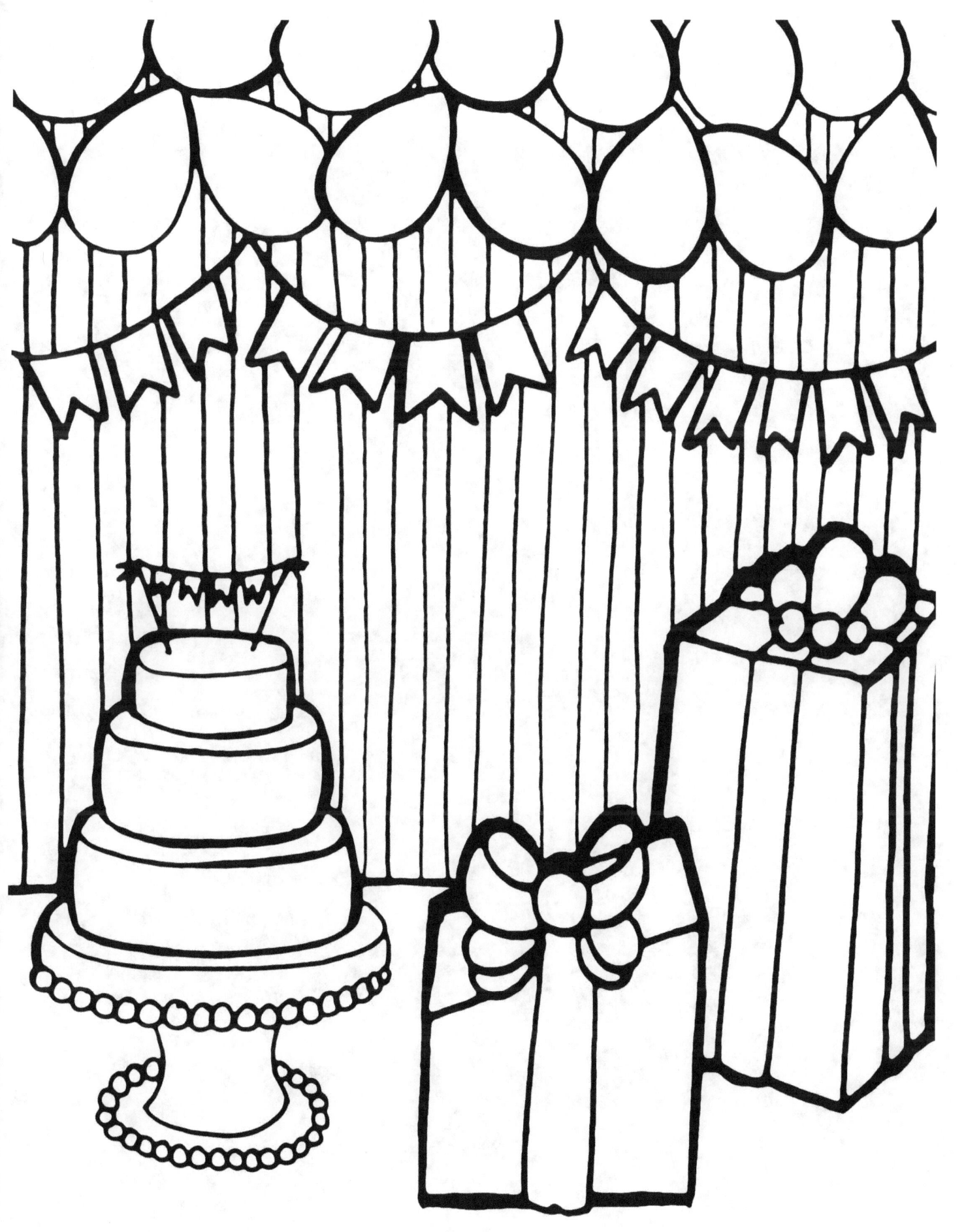

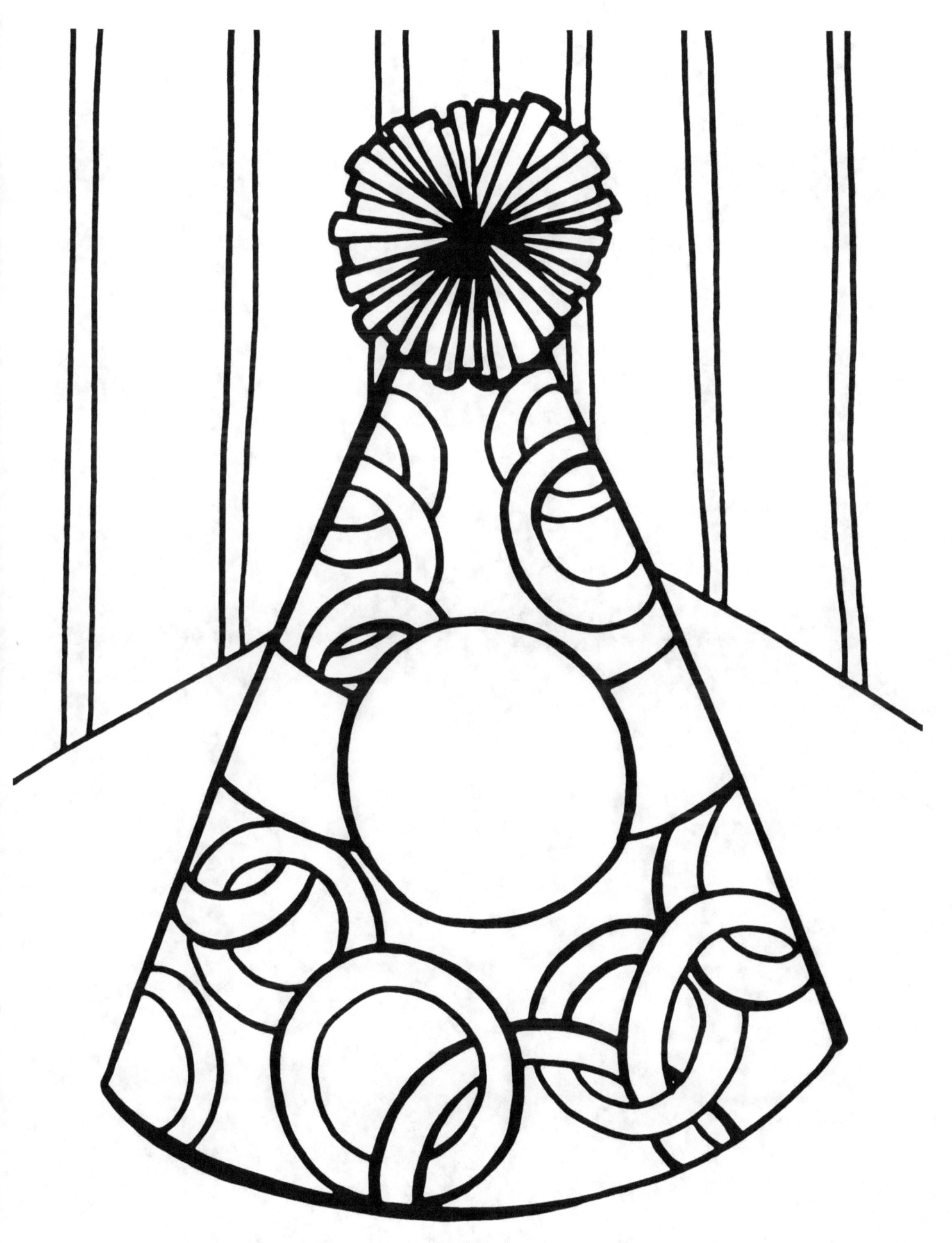

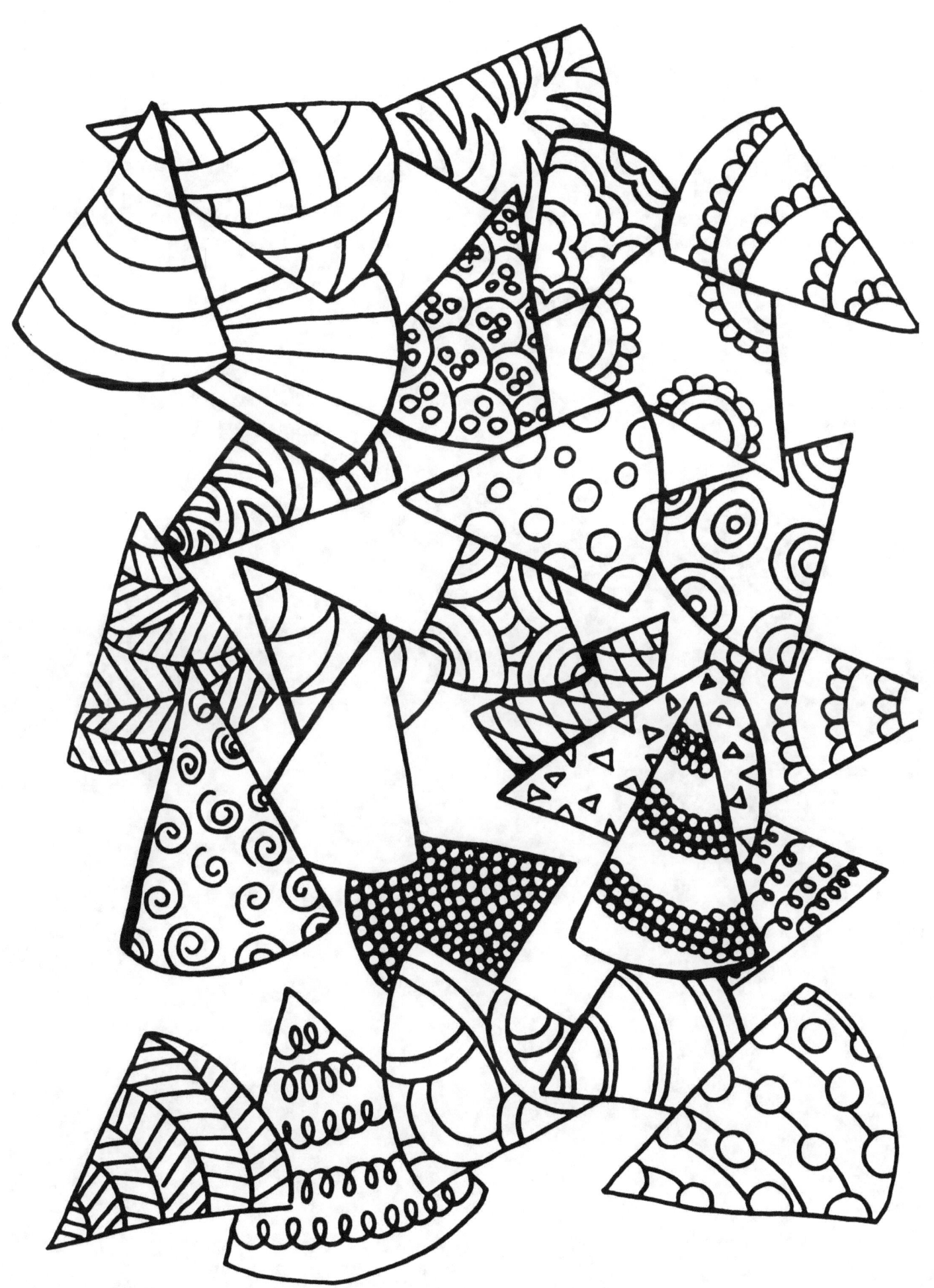

○ ○ ○ ○ ○ ○ ○ ○

Happy Birthday Happy Birthday

○ ○ ○ ○ ○ ○ ○ ○

Happy Birthday Happy Birthday

○ ○ ○ ○ ○ ○ ○ ○

Happy Birthday Happy Birthday

○ ○ ○ ○ ○ ○ ○ ○

Happy Birthday Happy Birthday

○ ○ ○ ○ ○ ○ ○ ○

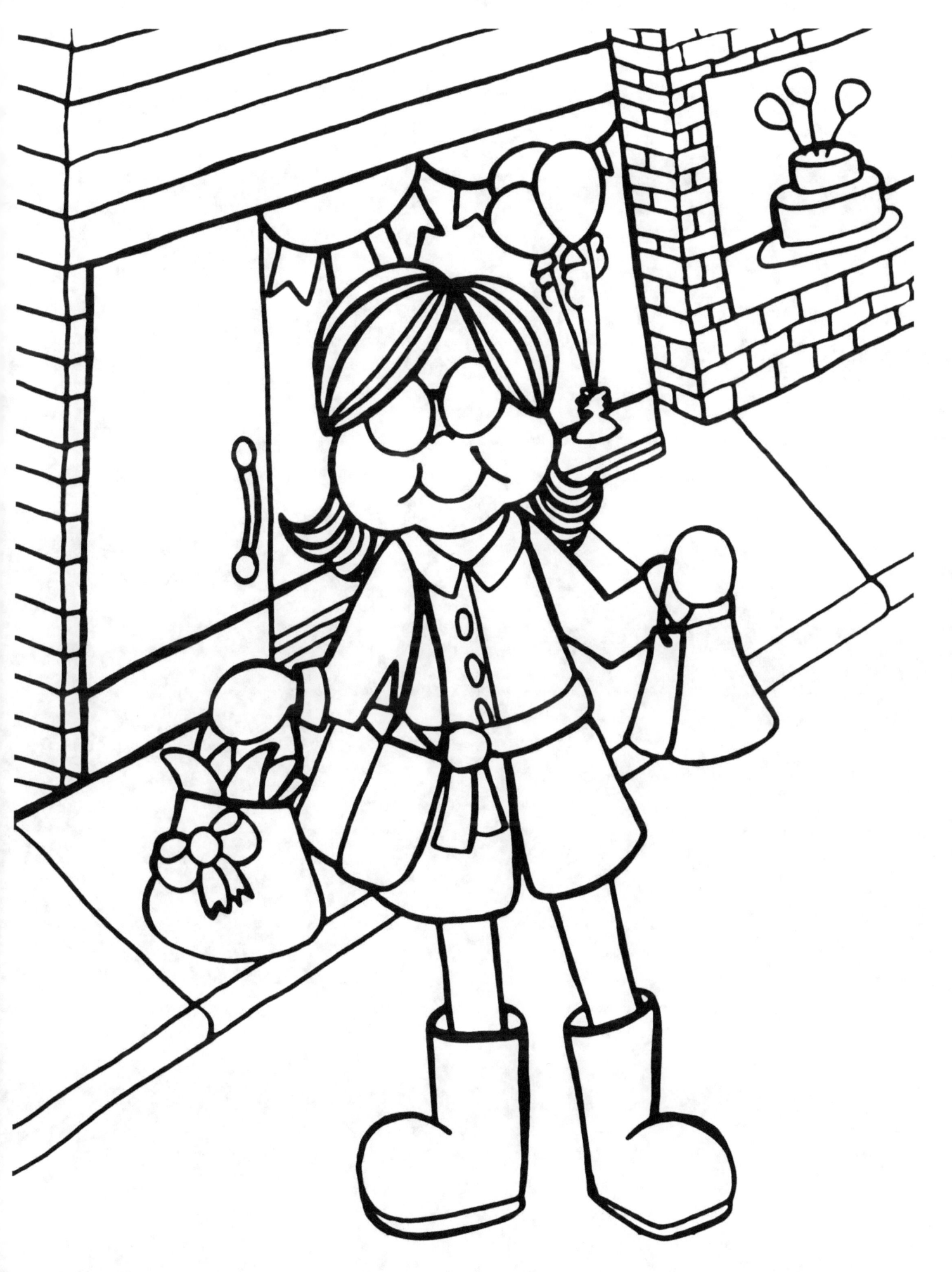

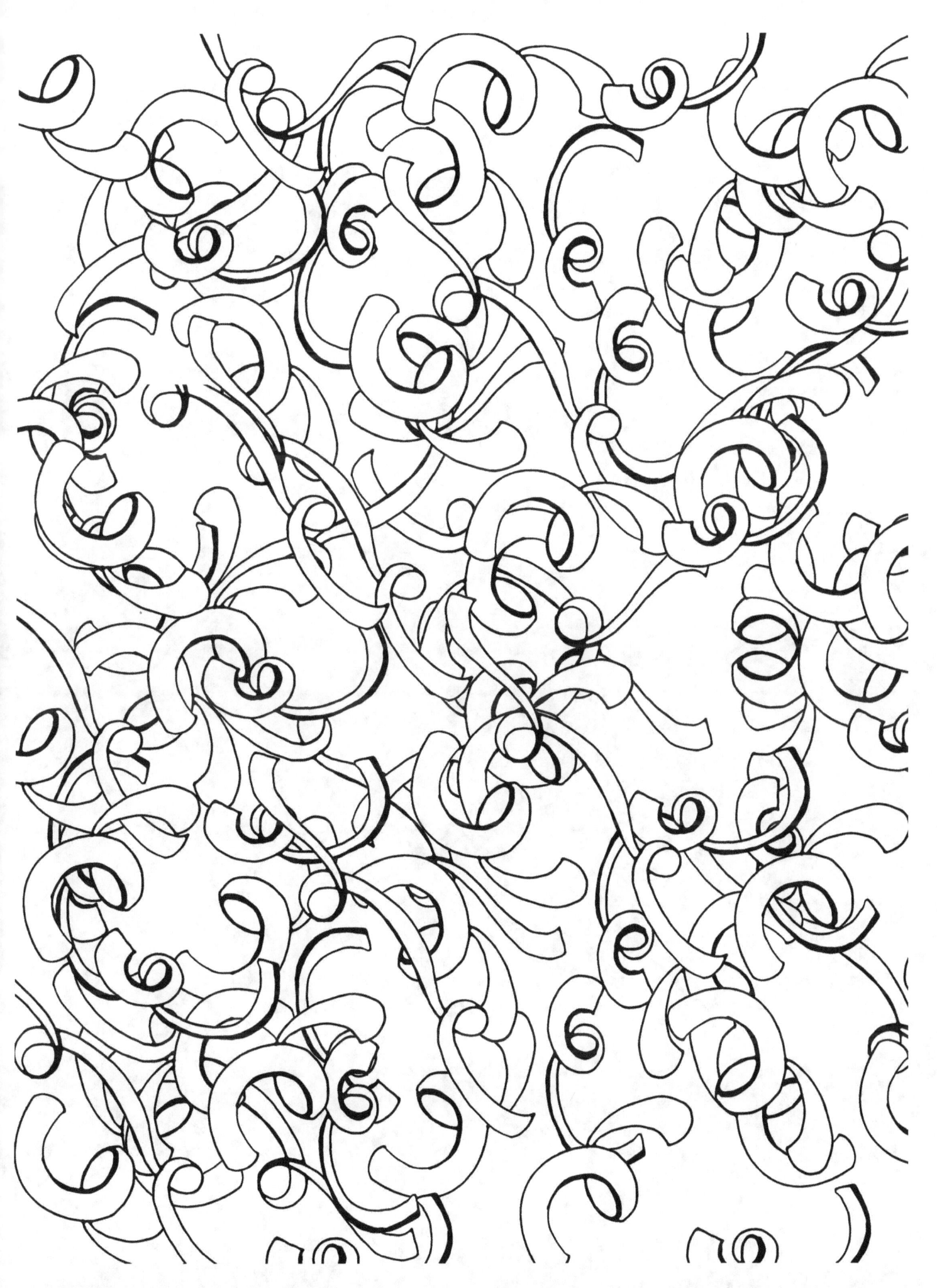

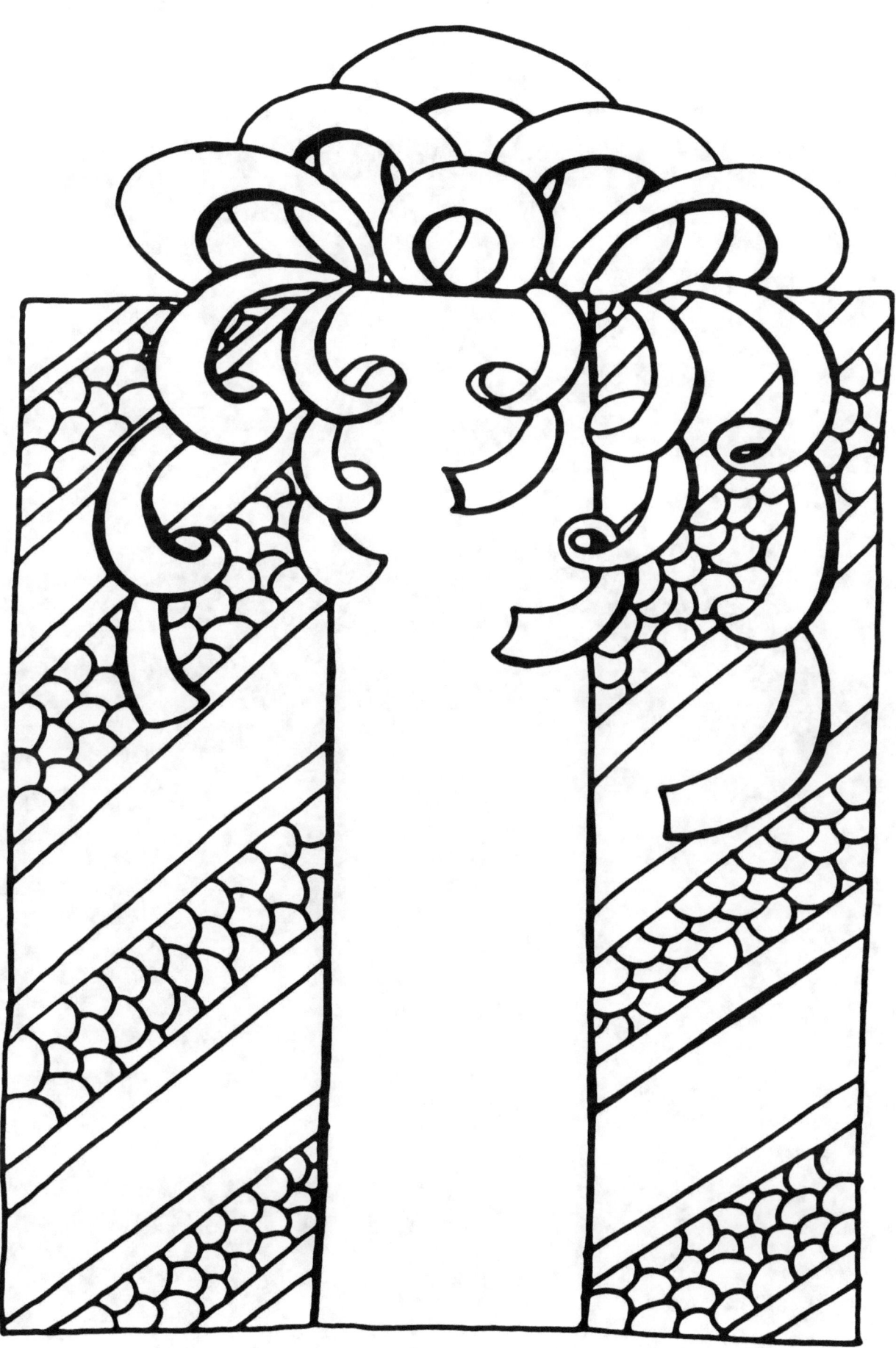

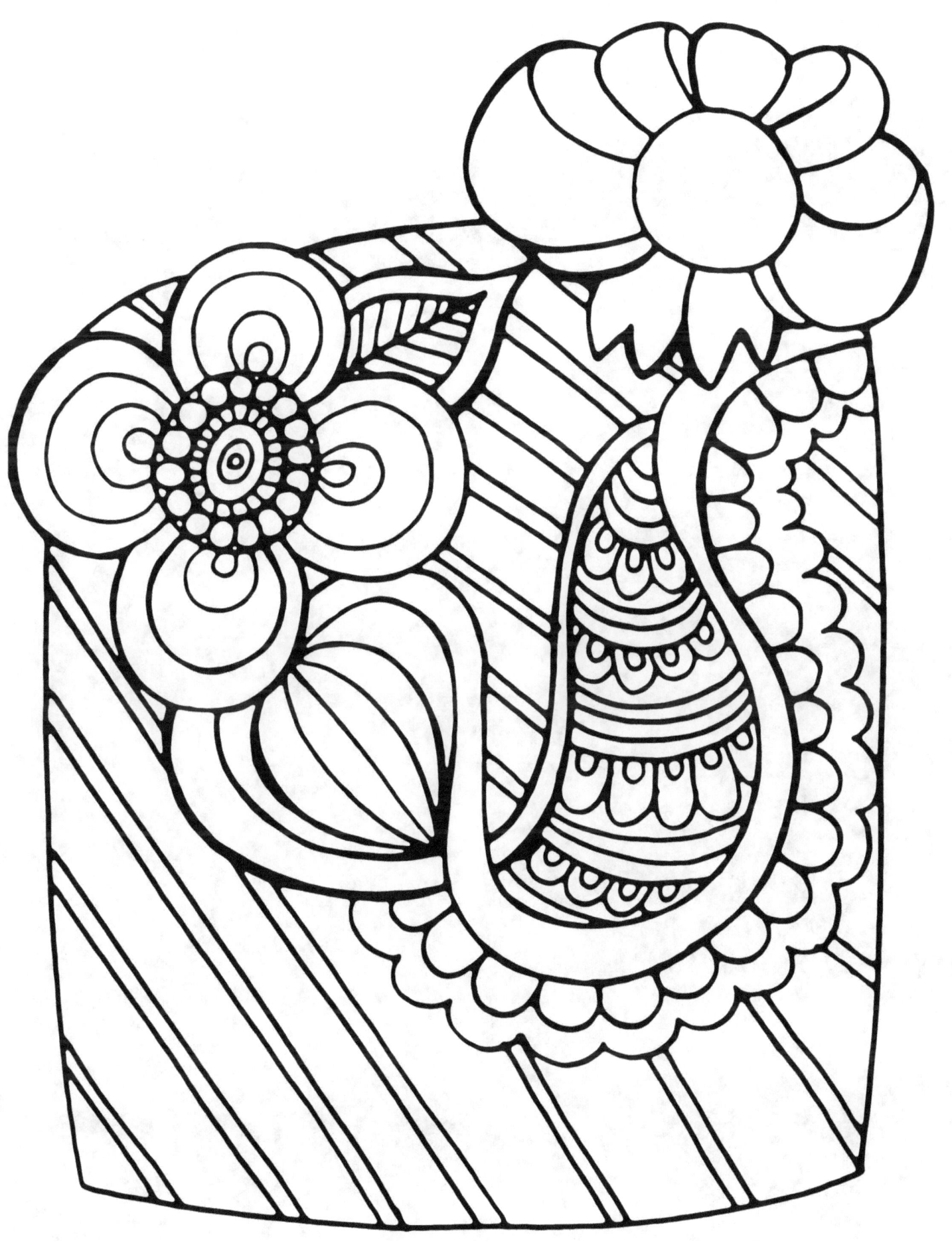

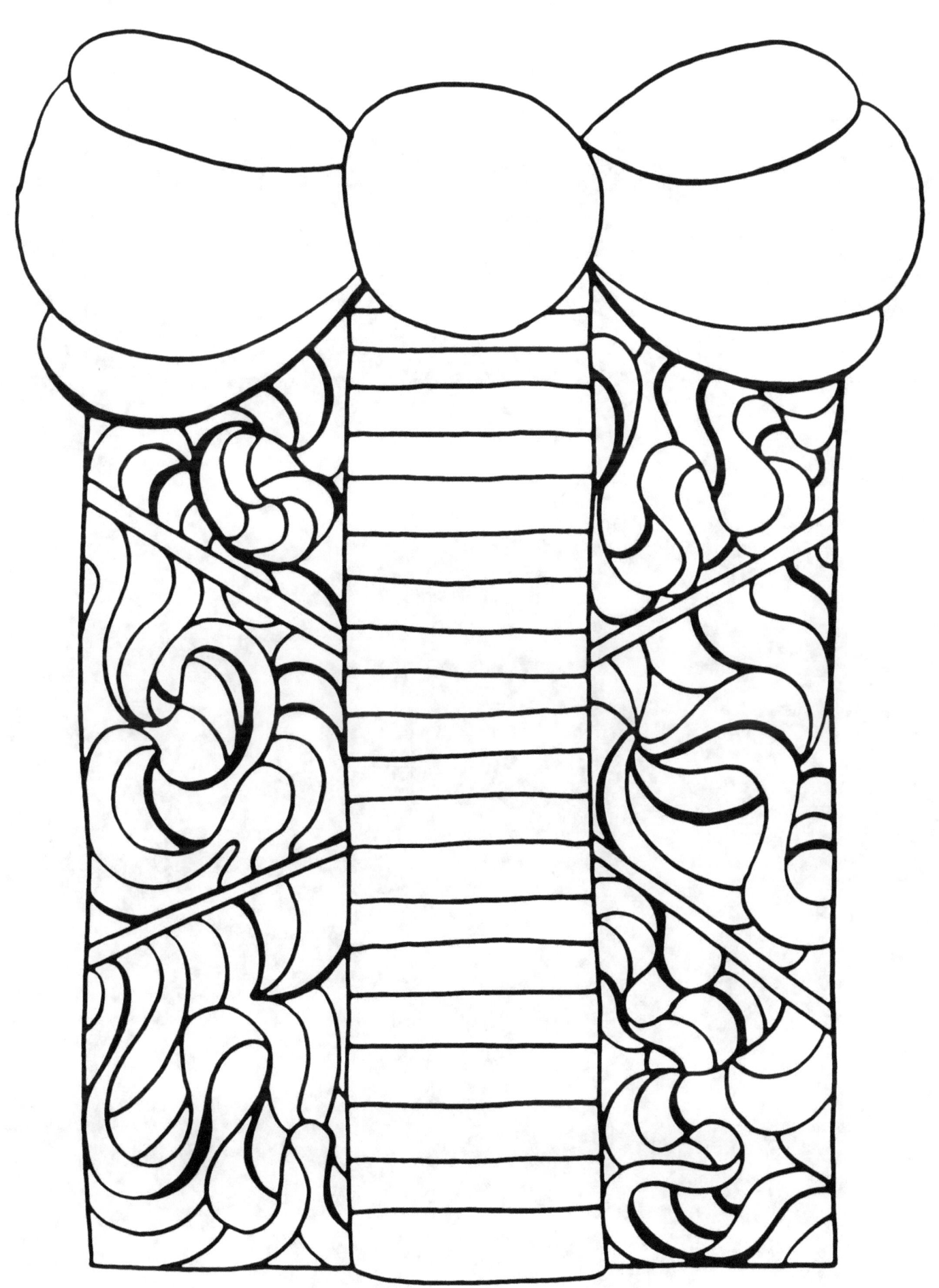

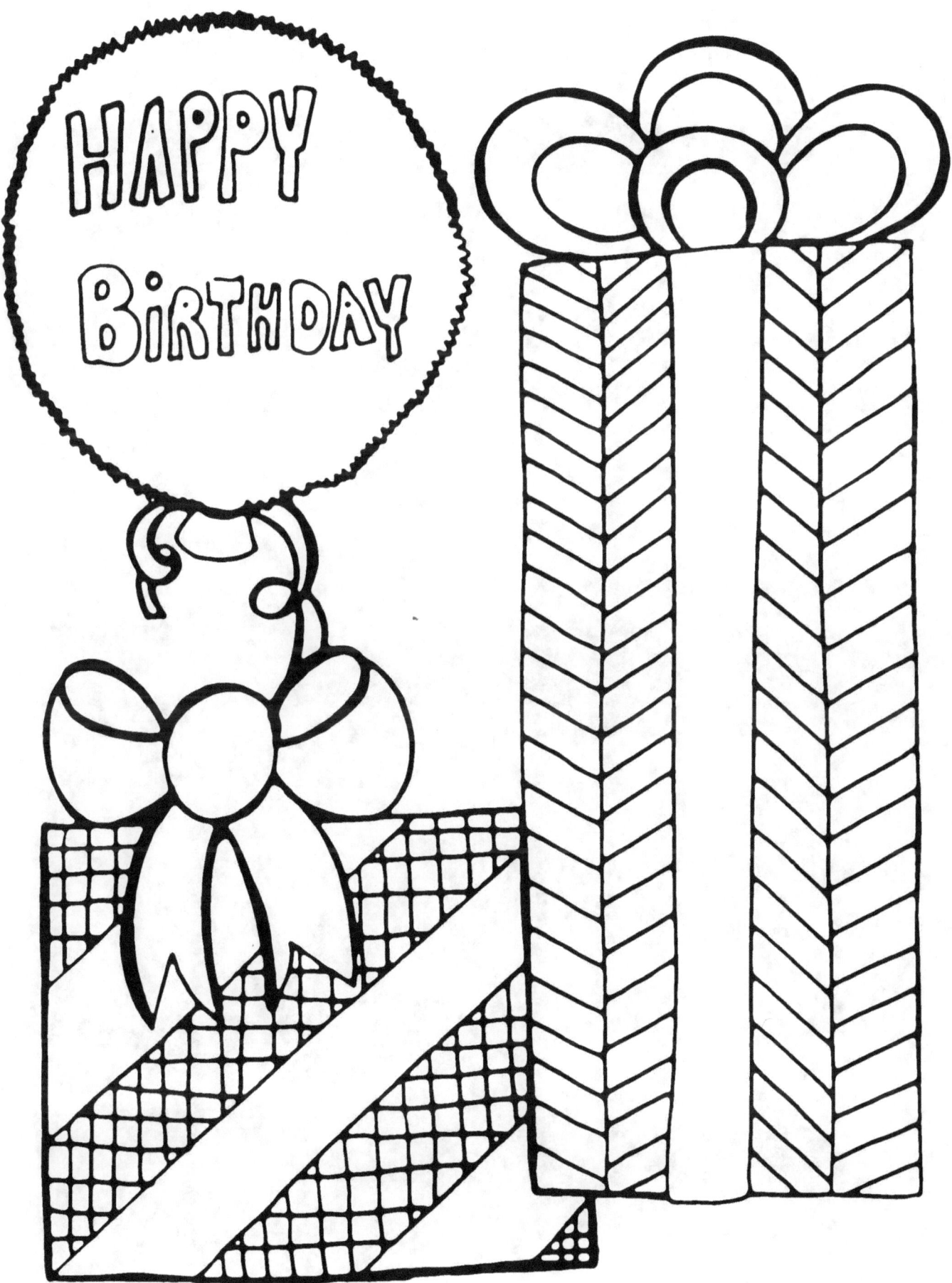

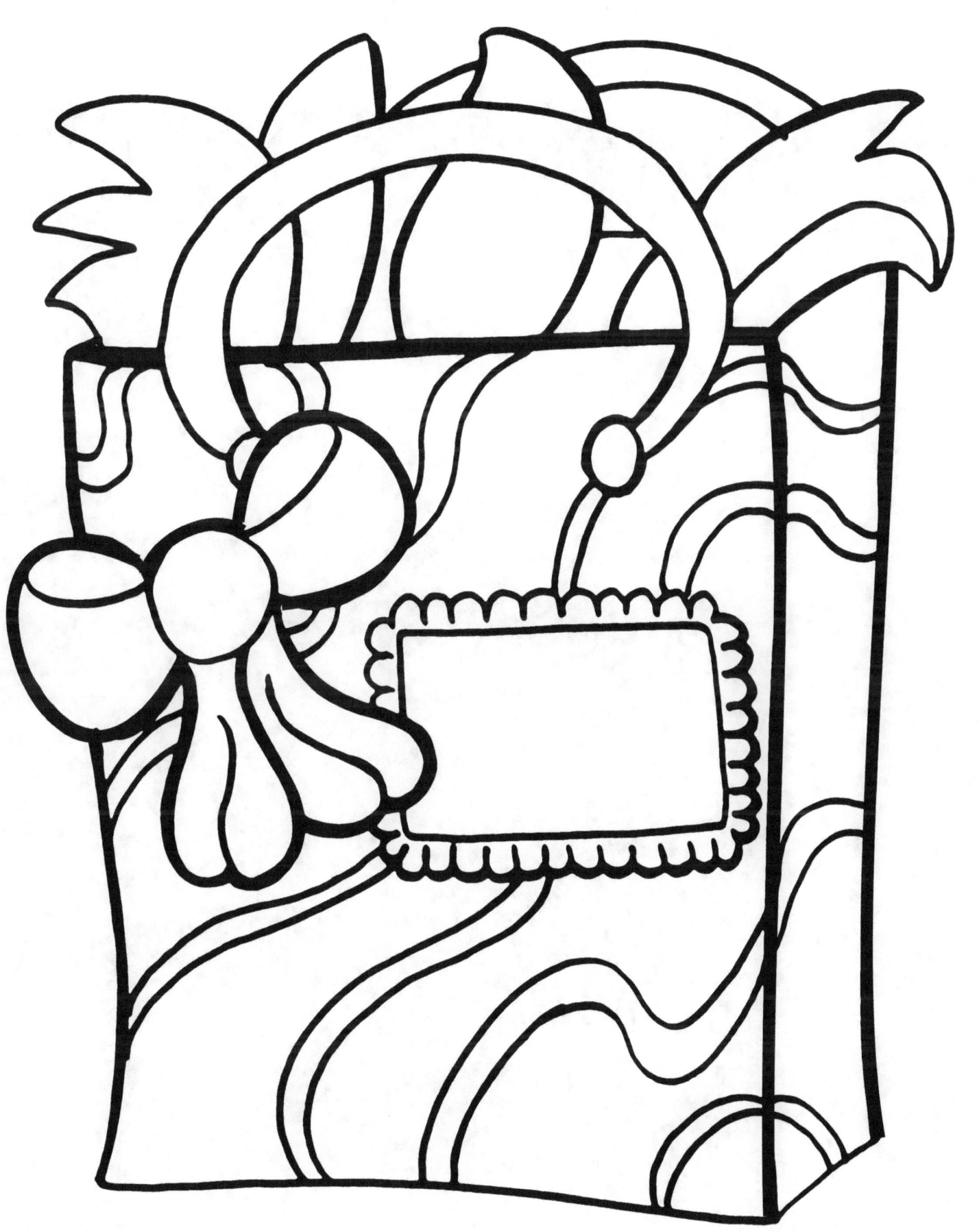

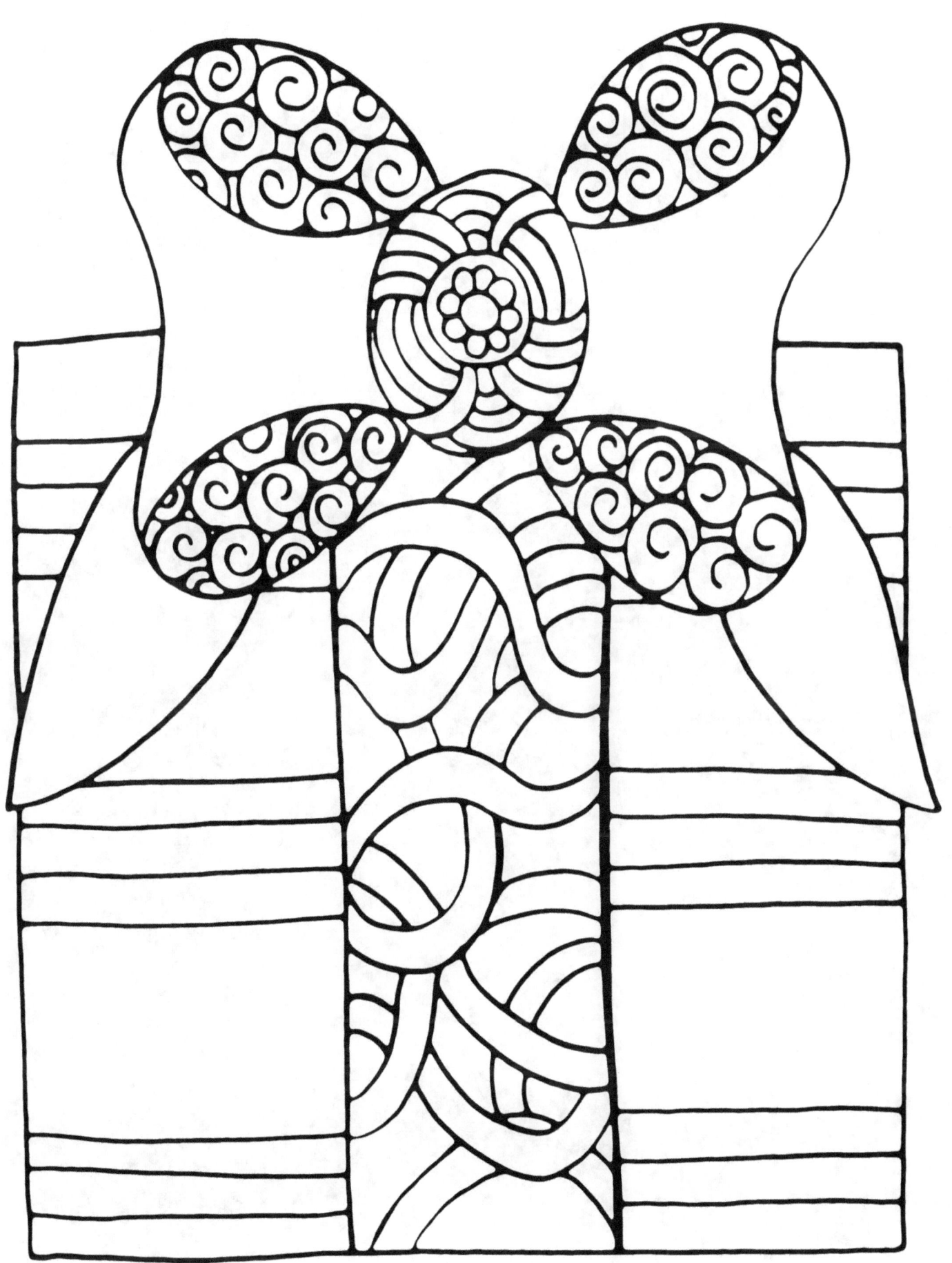

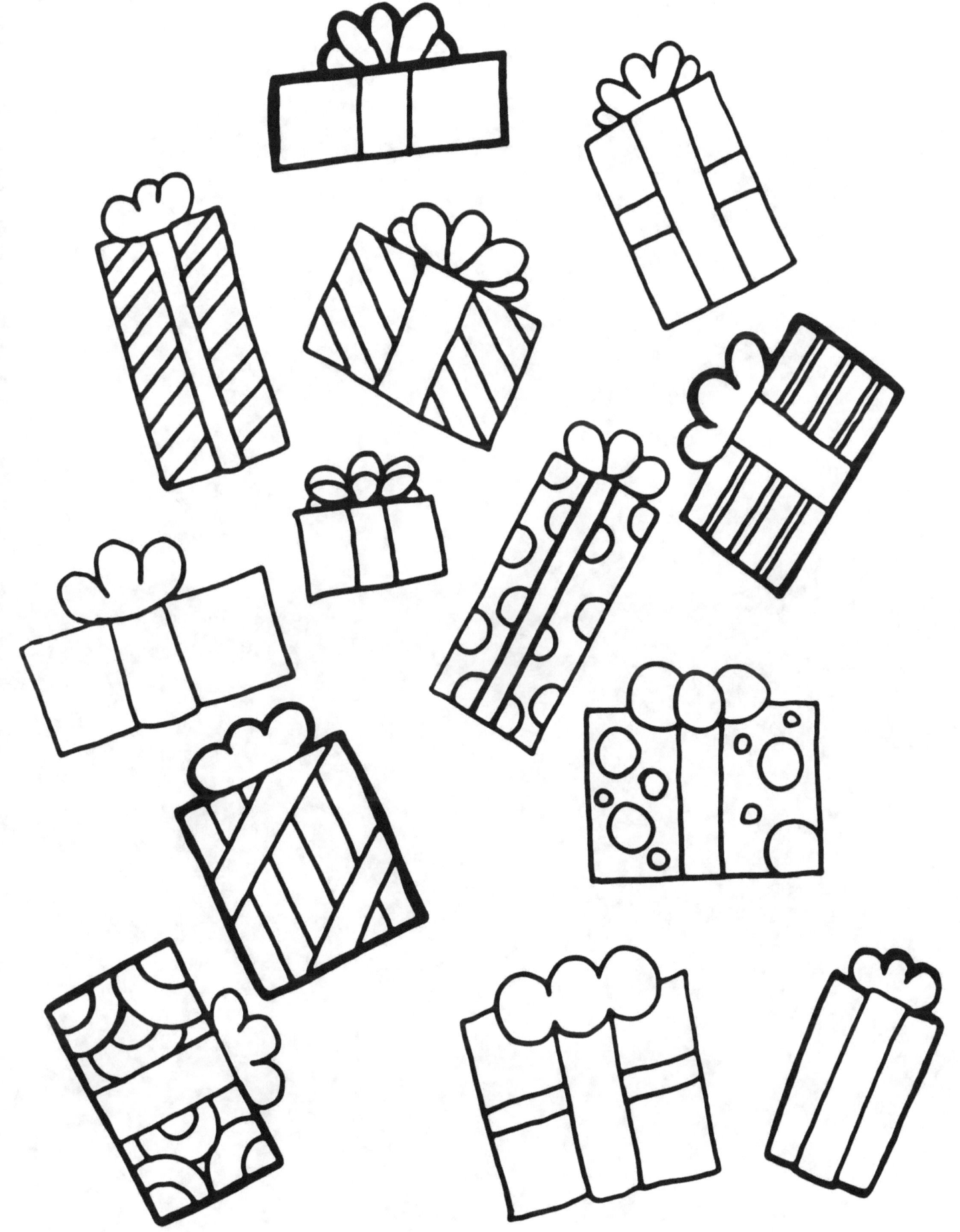

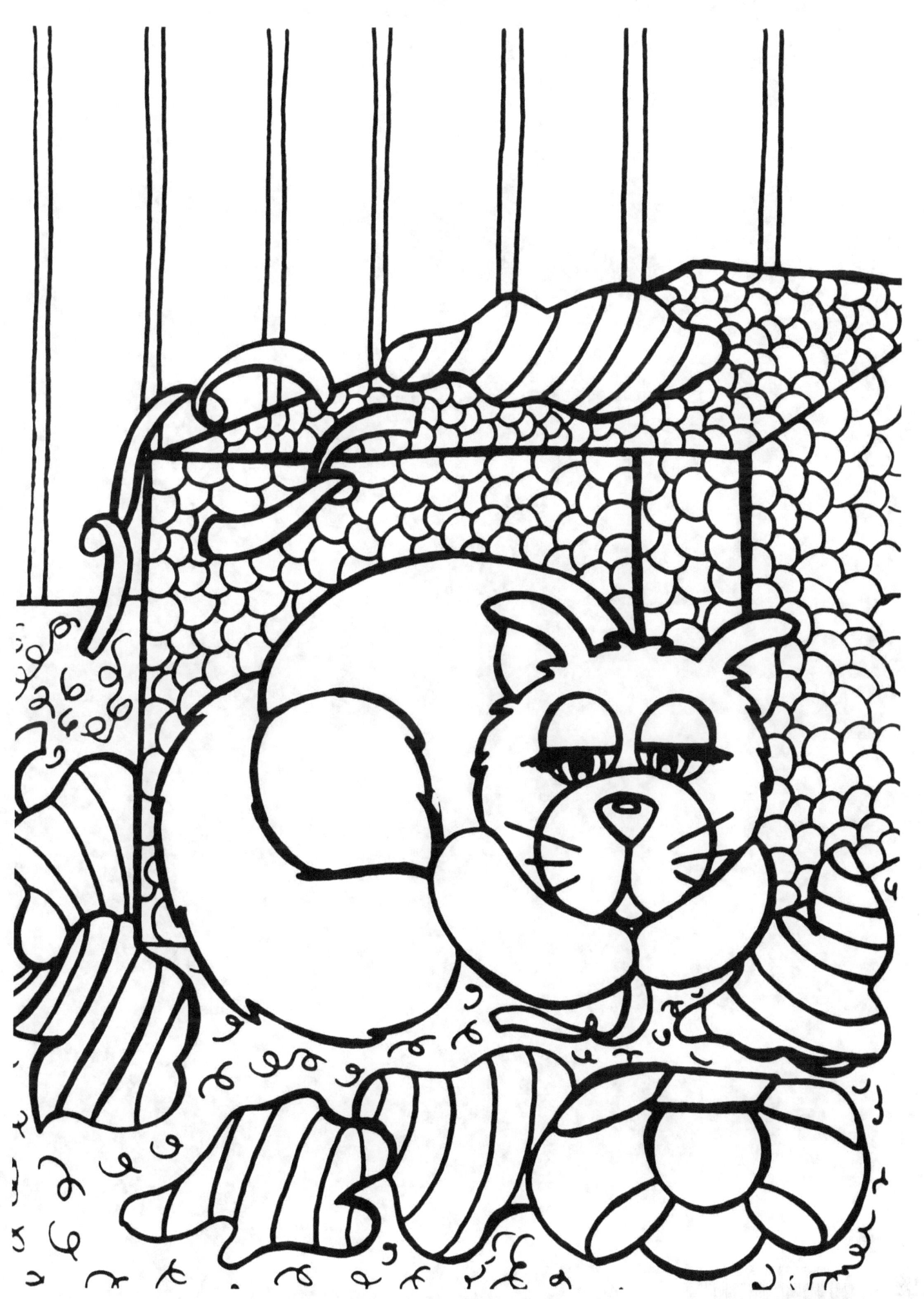